Amazon to Zami . . .

Cassell related titles:

Lesbiót: Israeli Lesbians Talk about Sexuality, Feminism Judaism and their Lives
Edited by Tracy Moore

Vamps, Virgins and Victims: How Can Women Fight AIDS?
Robin Gorna

My American History: Lesbian and Gay Life in the Reagan/Bush Years
Sarah Schulman

Hidden Holocaust?: Lesbian and Gay Persecution in Germany 1933–45
Gunter Grau with Claudia Schoppman

A Simple Matter of Justice?: Theorizing Lesbian and Gay Politics
Edited by Angela Wilson

True Stories of the Korean Comfort Women
Edited by Keith Howard

Surviving Indonesia's Gulag: A Western Woman's Prison Memoir
Carmel Budiardjo

Amazon to Zami

Towards a Global Lesbian Feminism

Edited by Monika Reinfelder

CASSELL PLC

CASSELL

Cassell plc
Wellington House
125 Strand
London WC2R 0BB

215 Park Avenue South
New York NY 10003

First published 1996

British Library Cataloguing-in-Publication Data
A catalogue record for this book is available from the British Library.

ISBN 0–304–33193 7 (hardback)
    0–304–33203 8 (paperback)

Typeset by York House Typographic Ltd, London

Printed and bound in Great Britain by Biddles Ltd, Guildford and King's Lynn

contents

*a*bout the *c*ontributors

CLAUDIA CSÖRNYEI

Lesbian feminist. Born in 1963 in La Plata (province of Buenos Aires, Argentina). Writer and teacher of literature and facilitator for writing workshops for women. She works as an editor and in computer-aided design (books, journals, magazines, posters, etc.). She is co-founder of the lesbian feminist group Las Lunas y Las Otras and of the Frente de Lesbianas de Buenos Aires.

GERTRUDE FESTER

Gertrude Fester is a 43-year-old black woman from Cape Town. She has been part of the anti-apartheid struggle and is a member of a number of South African women's organizations. A teacher by profession, she has been lecturing at the Hewat College of Education since 1982. She was detained in 1988 and charged with promoting the then banned African National Congress. During solitary confinement she started composing poetry, some of which has subsequently been published. Charges were withdrawn in March 1990. Gertrude is currently co-chair of the Women's National Coalition (Western Cape) and serves on several boards, including the state-subsidized Cape Performance Arts Board (CAPAB). She has written various articles on women. Her current interests are promoting the writing of women's struggle/history by participants themselves, and increasing South-South dialogue. She hopes to be able to study in a developing country in order to exchange and share strategies on the empowerment of black and marginalized women. She co-ordinated the NGO (non-governmental organization) activities in her province in preparation for the Fourth United Nations World Conference on Women in Beijing.

LIZ FRANK

Liz Frank writes textbooks and trains teachers. She is also a photographer and writes for the magazine *SISTER Namibia*. Making video films is next on her agenda. She lives in Windhoek with her lover and is learning to become a co-parent. She was active in raising lesbian visibility at the Fourth United Nations World Conference on Women in Beijing.

B.J.D. GAYATRI

B.J.D. Gayatri lives in Jakarta, Indonesia. She teaches psychology at the Jakarta Institute of Arts and is co-founder and member of a sexuality research group. She is editor of the only lesbian newsletter and journal in Indonesia. When time permits she also works as a copywriter, graphic designer and photographer. She is a member of the International Advisory Board of IGLHRC (International Gay and Lesbian Human Rights Commission).

ELIZABETH KHAXAS

Elizabeth Khaxas is a teacher, writer and student. She is also a feminist community activist and a lover of women. She lives with her lover in Windhoek and is a loving parent. Her poetry has appeared in an anthology of women's writing published by the SISTER Namibia Collective of which she is a member.

TINA MACHIDA

Tina Machida had to leave college when her parents found out about her sexuality and refused to pay for her education. She is co-founder of an income-generating and housing project for lesbians in Harare, for which she is seeking financial donors. She is also a member of GALZ (Gays and Lesbians in Zimbabwe). Tina has a daughter aged thirteen whom she adopted when the girl's lesbian mother died.

ROSE MARY MADDEN ARIAS

Rose Mary Madden Arias was born in Costa Rica. She is a feminist lawyer who tries to defend the rights of women in an androcentric and heterosexual legal system. She was the legal representative of a group of women musicians who play non-sexist songs; and she is a member of the Latin

American and Caribbean network Cladem that works for women's rights. She was a founder member of the lesbian feminist group Las Entendidas, and has participated in the Costa Rican, Central American and Latin American feminist movement, in human rights conferences and at the Fourth United Nations Conference on Women in Beijing.

MALU MARIN

Malu Lourdes S. Marin works as a writer, researcher, desktop publisher and trainer. She is co-founder of CLIC (Can't Live in the Closet!), a lesbian group with an evolving character. It publishes the newsletter *Breakout* and aims to undertake anthropological and historical research on lesbianism in the Philippines. Currently the group is engaged in research on lesbianism and the law. In addition it is a research centre for print and audiovisual materials on lesbian issues. Malu is also a member of KALAYAAN (Liberation), a feminist collective founded in 1983. She is involved in a Dream group. Her sun sign is Aquarius (rising sign Taurus, moon sign Aries), and she was born in the Year of the Monkey.

RAIS NUR (pseudonym)

Rais Nur is an androgynous Malaysian lesbian feminist. She studied abroad for seven years and has been working in Malaysia with different women's groups since 1992. She considers herself a fairly out lesbian; the extent of her outness being subject to family constraints (actually, just her mother!). While acknowledging that it is a privilege to be out to friends and colleagues and continue to remain accepted, she also believes very much in the need to be out in order to start shattering the myths and misconceptions of lesbianism in Malaysia. She hopes to see a feminist and lesbian movement in her country one day, but realizes that this will be difficult since oppressive circumstances have forced other like-minded lesbian feminists abroad. Nevertheless, she believes that there are still enough local lesbians left to work towards this goal. She would like to make more time to learn, to meet more lesbians and to attend to her plants.

SILVIA PALUMBO

Lesbian feminist. Born in 1963 in Lincoln (province of Buenos Aires, Argentina). Composer of Latin American popular music. Chair of the Taller de Canciones (song workshop) at the Cultural Centre of the University of

Buenos Aires. She performs in pubs and underground cafés. She also teaches swimming to people with disabilities. Silvia has participated in the feminist movement since 1988. She is co-founder of the feminist lesbian group Las Lunas y Las Otras and of the Frente de Lesbianas de Buenos Aires. Her main wish is to see Latin America and the Caribbean invaded by music created by their women and for them.

A.R. (pseudonym)

A.R. has a BA in English Literature from Durham University and an MA in English and Women's Studies from Lancaster University in the UK. She returned to Malaysia in 1994 having lived abroad for the previous ten years; and since then has been attempting to reintegrate herself into Malaysian society. She is a journalist by profession and a volunteer at a Kuala Lumpur-based women's NGO. Having come out in the UK, where she fashioned a sense of identity as a lesbian feminist, the transition to Malaysia has proved quite shocking at times, especially in terms of the role-play among lesbians. However, she feels very fortunate to be familiar with two such different cultures and feels that she has learned a lot from both. She is very committed to promoting feminism and lesbian rights in Malaysia, and is especially optimistic about the local arts and theatre scene, which she perceives as very dynamic and having great potential for consciousness-raising. Other passions include flirting indiscriminately, writing mawkish poetry and combing Malaysian bookshops for that rare thing, a lesbian book.

MONIKA REINFELDER

Monika Reinfelder teaches Women's Studies and Politics at the University of London. Of German working-class origin, she has lived and travelled widely in Latin America and Africa. She is active in the international lesbian feminist movement, has participated in many international lesbian and women's conferences, and writes on sexuality, class, race and gender. Her favourite people/things are (some) lesbians, palm trees and *la musica salsa*.

CONSUELO RIVERA FUENTES

Consuelo Rivera Fuentes was involved in opposition politics during the dictatorship in Chile. After the return to 'democracy' she founded the lesbian feminist group LEA (Lesbianas En Acción) based in Concepción.

At present she is at Lancaster University in the UK, carrying out research for her PhD thesis on the social construction of lesbian identities through the analysis of unpublished autobiographies and oral accounts. In her spare time she is an activist of her dreams, a mother and a lover. She is the author of a book of poetry, *La Liberación de La Eva Desgarrada*, and has published two collective poetry books with the Chilean literary group Mujer (Woman) in Concepción. She also shares some of her poetry in English with other like-minded dreamers in the Lancaster women's writers' collection *Women's Words*.

GITI THADANI

Giti Thadani is a founding member and co-ordinator of Sakhi, the Lesbian Resource Centre in New Delhi, India. In 1993, she organized the first seminar in the history of alternative sexualities in South Asia. Giti is a writer and photographer who travels extensively in India, documenting archetypes of the cosmic Feminine. She is currently working on a book, *Sakhiyani: Genealogies of Lesbian Desire*.

introduction: weaving international webs

monika reinfelder

Since the late 1980s a vibrant lesbian feminist activism has been emerging in Latin America and the Caribbean, Asia and the Pacific Islands, and to a lesser extent in Africa. And yet, the old myth of lesbianism being an exclusively Western phenomenon remains strongly. Very few of us have access to the ideas and struggles of lesbians in non-Western countries. The literature available on lesbian theory and activism focuses on North American and North European lesbians. Most of it is written by, and documents the lives of, White[1] lesbians. A few texts are available by Black, Asian, Pacific Islander, Latina and Chicana lesbians living in North America and the UK,[2] and texts on Chinese and Arab lesbians in the USA and writings by lesbians in Eastern Europe are in the pipeline. But apart from an anthology on lesbians in Israel and two on lesbian and gay lives in South Africa,[3] the writings of Latin American, Caribbean, Asian, Pacific Islander and African lesbians have not yet made their way into the mainstream publishing world. As a Peruvian lesbian comments:

> When I speak of my right to my own culture and language as an indigenous woman, everyone agrees to my self-determination. But when I speak of my other identity, my lesbian identity, my right to love, to determine my own sexuality, no one wants to listen.[4]

This is a particularly notable omission in the rapid expansion of the 'Women and Development' literature that has taken place over the last few years. Gender perspectives on 'development', structural adjustment, the environment, population, illiteracy, poverty, etc., have been offered by many writers. However, except for a few isolated references to lesbians, almost the entire output of this literature assumes all women to be heterosexual. Lesbians are yet again made invisible. Their existence is denied, either implicitly or explicitly.

This denial is damaging for lesbians in non-Western countries, and bewildering for those of us from the West who have lived with lesbians in such countries and have, upon our arrival, spent days, weeks, even months, before knowingly meeting a heterosexual woman. Of course, many lesbians are not open about their sexuality in public. This applies in particular to those who hold prestigious posts and live in the public eye. As the feminist journal *SISTER Namibia* comments:

> Lesbians in Namibia find their situation very hard because there is much prejudice against alternative relationships and little realisation that lesbianism has existed throughout the history of the human race, and is therefore not so 'foreign' as many Namibians would like to believe.[5]

The editorial of *SISTER Namibia* 'is committed to the elimination of gender oppression, racism, homophobia and other issues that oppress and divide women'.

The anti-lesbianism in most countries is as rife as it is in the UK. After publicly outing herself, TV celebrity Sandi Toksvig was sacked from the Save the Children Fund (UK) because of her sexuality at the same time as two lesbians in the Philippines lost their jobs at a human rights organization. There are numerous parallels to be drawn. But the mushrooming of lesbian groups in Latin American, Caribbean, African, Asian and Pacific Islander countries testifies to the fact that lesbians are no longer prepared to live in the closet, a sentiment that is expressed succinctly in the name of the Filipina lesbian group CLIC: Can't Live in the Closet!

However, many women-loving women do not use the label 'lesbian' (or the equivalent term in their country). A study in the USA found that 60 per cent of women who have sexual relationships with women do not identify as lesbians.[6] In other countries, either the Western connotation or the danger the term can bring with itself often leads to the use of the term 'women-loving women' or the euphemistic 'independent women', 'single [sic] women' and 'women who are not attached to men'.[7] In Maori culture it is recognized that women who are 'like that' have existed since time immemorial and form an integrated part of their community. And indigenous peoples in North America often revered women who had same-sex relationships.[8] In other cases lack of awareness of labels, or even of the existence of other women with the same experiences, will ensure not only an absence of identification but also extreme levels of loneliness, a situation discussed by many of this anthology's authors.

Many women lead a heterosexual existence as well as having women lovers. This is often tolerated, as two women are not perceived to be capable of having sex with each other. Sex is identified with the penis and is therefore not seen as possible in the absence of a man. As long as the women involved are in heterosexual marriages and are prepared to have children, no harm is seen in two women sleeping together. The absence of a label that can be used against women can protect their ability to relate to each other sexually. In some cultures marriage between women is an accepted practice. Sometimes these marriages are for purely reproductive reasons and are not necessarily sexual: an infertile woman may take a younger 'wife' who will bear her children. In other cases, however, the relationship has an obvious sexual character. Beverley Ditsie from FLOW (Feminist Lesbians of Witwatersrand) argues that in her culture in South Africa

> the traditional leader is a queen, who always had wives. A queen could have 10 or 20 wives. It seems that the more we get educated or 'civilized', the more the generations want to close down our herstory. The only explanation I can think of is that this is a fear of female power.[9]

In other South African societies, women who are healers are exempt from heterosexual marriage and are allowed to marry other women. In Zimbabwe, as Tina Machida explains (see Chapter eight), women who want to marry other women have to prove to be in possession of a male spirit, yet another example of how female autonomy is perceived as an impossibility. If the woman has no penis, at least she has to have a male spirit! But even in these female unions, reproduction, women's main function in heteropatriarchal[10] society, as well as the provision of sexual services to men, are still expected. Her wives reproduce by being impregnated by a man, not through self-insemination. And her marriage is supposed to follow the heterosexual model of polygyny.

The label 'lesbian' is predominantly used by those who have proudly taken on a lesbian identity. In many countries it is feminists in particular who use the term. For them their sexuality is not merely a preference, it is also a political issue. In the words of two Western feminists: 'Categories of oppressed people are not well served by denying the existence of the categories to which they belong: at the very least, such denial refuses a name for the oppressed and militates against collective resistance.'[11] It is precisely the theme of collective resistance that runs like a common thread through the articles in this book. The authors' lesbian feminist politics set them at odds not only with the 'establishment' but also with the heterosexual women's movement and the gay movement in their countries, within which they found themselves fighting anti-lesbianism and misogyny respectively.

Recognizing the dangers of definitions I can only offer a working definition of lesbian feminism. Lesbians,[12] according to Malu Marin, are 'women who choose to direct their energies to other women, emotionally, physically, sexually, politically and spiritually, amongst other things'. Feminism takes on different forms,[13] but in the case of lesbian feminism it is an analysis of the oppression of women, in particular lesbian women, and an action that aims at the transformation of power structures based on sexuality, disability, cast, class, race and gender. Lesbian feminism, unlike other forms of feminism, sees the institution of heterosexuality as one, if not *the*, cornerstone of oppression.[14]

The title *Amazon to Zami* captures the spirit of the book. Amazons, the ancient mythical warriors who fought for a women-identified culture, were perhaps not dissimilar to present-day activists, except in their choice of weapons. Zami is used by Black women who do not like the White association of the term lesbian. It originates from the Caribbean island of Carriacou and refers to women-loving women. There are words for women-loving women starting with almost every letter of the alphabet and belonging to many different languages. The most internationally known are lesbian, dyke, Zami, wicker, mati, khush, *entendidas*. Examples of words that have not yet crossed many national borders are *sakhi, suhak, jami*. Some of these terms are discussed by the authors, who explore the history, myths, oppression and celebration of lesbians in their respective countries and relate current lesbian existence and actions to the pressing political issues of their region.

Malu Marin links the absence of documented lesbian history in the Philippines to Spanish colonization, and discusses the effects of fundamentalist Catholicism on positive lesbian identity. She looks at the relationship between politically active lesbian feminists and non-feminist lesbians. The chapter concludes with an example of anti-lesbian employment discrimination. Unfortunately, she did not as yet have access to the research conducted by Lesbond (a Baguio-based lesbian feminist organization) on indigenous lesbians in the provinces of Cordillera.

Giti Thadani looks at the myth of a 'women-centred' culture in India within which 'homosocial' and 'homoemotive' behaviour is more accept-able than 'heterosocial' and 'heteroemotive' behaviour. That is, it is more acceptable for women to socialize and express affection with each other than it is between men and women. This women centredness is only acceptable, however, as long as it takes place within the framework of heterosexuality. Open lesbian identity, public homoerotic and homo-sexual behaviour is unacceptable. Thadani links poverty and lack of economic development to the institution of heterosexuality that relegates women to the private sphere with no control over resources. Her chapter points to the contradiction in Indian society where lesbianism is declared non-existent and yet had to be illegalized in the past. It concludes with a description of a nascent lesbian feminist activism, in particular in the form of the Sakhi network and its Jami project, an attempt to excavate the rich archaeological history of female erotic relationships in India.

Rais Nur and AR discuss the difficulty of constructing a lesbian identity in Malaysia, which they see as heavily influenced by factors such as class, ethnicity and religion. They focus on how women's sexuality generally, and lesbian sexuality specifically, is controlled and regulated by the state. Their article analyses the effects of secular and Islamic laws on lesbians, the social sanctions, and the lack of support from heterosexual women's groups.

BJD Gayatri questions a 'culture' that is opposed to feminism on the basis that it is Western, while uncritically and enthusiastically embracing TV, technology (in particular reproductive technology harmful to women), Kentucky Fried Chicken, Pizza Hut and McDonald's, all clearly alien to Indonesia. In her country the word lesbian has such negative connotations that even terms like 'dyke' or 'queer' are safer to use. Gayatri assesses the role of the media in constructing negative images and stereotypes of lesbians that are also reproduced in the women's movement.

South Africa occupies the unique position of being the first and only country in the world in which discrimination based on sexual orientation is unconstitutional. This is the result of the work of lesbian and gay rights activists in the anti-apartheid movement. Gertrude Fester analyses the history and relationship between those two movements and the struggle to include sexual orientation in the interim constitution. She provides an insight into the election campaign, the post-election period, and the race and class implications for lesbian politics. She also issues a warning that whatever has been gained cannot be taken for granted. Much work is yet to be done to combat lesbian oppression and to keep sexual orientation in the final constitution of South Africa when it comes into effect in May 1996.

In bordering Namibia Liz Frank and Elizabeth Khaxas look with admiration at the South African lesbian and gay movement, a movement which has only just started in Namibia. They miss a lesbian subculture in Windhoek and long for places where they can meet other lesbians, exchange experiences, information, literature or just celebrate with other women. But they do ask themselves the question if, as a Black and White lesbian couple, they are not better off in the new Namibia, given the growing racism in Europe.[15] Lesbians are beginning to assert themselves and take on the challenge of creating new values in a new Namibia. The authors 'discover' the existence of lesbians in Namibia in the 1920s, discuss the attitude of the South West African People's Organization (SWAPO) to lesbians, and relate the situation of lesbians to the oppression of women in general. They challenge the assumption that only women's poverty and women's needs in health and education merit political attention by arguing that 'standing up for lesbian rights takes no butter off anybody's bread' and that lesbians are found in every community, including those in poverty and in need of health and education. They believe that the time has come to speak out as lesbians in their community and country, and see it as a challenge to 'research lesbianism in the past and present in the diverse communities of Namibia'.

The situation is even more difficult in Zimbabwe, with a president who calls upon citizens to arrest lesbians and gay men (see p. 115). In the face of such oppression Tina Machida's article is a testimony to lesbian survival and strength. The day-to-day struggles of Black unemployed working-class lesbians render feminist theory a luxury, but their active resistance to heteropatriarchy puts the most ardent of feminists to shame. Machida describes the extreme abuse she and other lesbians had to endure because of their sexuality. White supremacy in Zimbabwe has left a legacy of high unemployment and poverty, and with no family or state support poor Black lesbians often have no other alternative than prostitution. The income-generating co-operative, of which Machida is a founding member, provides not only alternative sources of income but also accommodation for homeless lesbians, albeit in overcrowded conditions. In Machida's experience her White lesbian friends face less oppression from their families than her Black friends and she herself have endured. Without wanting to deny her experience, however, this is not a position that can be generalized. Black lesbian writers in the USA and the UK have identified anti-lesbianism as a phenomenon equally rampant in the Black and White communities.[16] Nevertheless, it is a situation that affects Black lesbians more, as they are dependent on their community for support against racism. The explanation of Machida's experience lies in the economic class position of her White friends' families that provides them with the ability to 'buy' respect and allows more access to liberal education on issues of sexuality, as well as in their racism, according to which a White lesbian is still preferable to a Black heterosexual. Her appeal to the international community for support could (and should) become a challenge to the emerging international lesbian feminist movement.

Like lesbians in Africa recently, Latin American lesbians have been networking across national boundaries since the early 1980s. A member of the network, Rose Mary Madden Arias, tells the story of the formation of the first lesbian feminist group, Las Entendidas, in Costa Rica. She relates their somewhat amusing, but also frightening, encounter with the forces of reaction in Costa Rica (most notably the Catholic Church) when organizing the Second Latin American and Caribbean Lesbian Feminist *Encuentro* (conference) in 1990, a 'strange event' according to a national newspaper.

Unaware of the formation of the Latin American and Caribbean lesbian network in Mexico in 1987, Consuelo Rivera Fuentes suffered the loneliness, isolation and confusion of most young lesbians. She takes us through the journey of her self-recognition as a lesbian, living through the horrors of the dictatorship in Chile. She also documents lesbian survival, resistance and celebration in the form of the two Chilean lesbian groups, *Ayuquelen* in Santiago and LEA (Lesbianas En Acción – Lesbians in Action) in Concepción.

A few years later Silvia Palumbo and Claudia Csörnyei were very busy organizing the Fourth Latin American and Caribbean Lesbian Feminist *Encuentro* in Argentina, April 1995, while writing their chapter. The preparations for this event, as well as those for the Fourth United Nations World Conference on Women in Beijing, have made clear the variety of perspectives expressed by Latin American and Caribbean lesbians and posed the question of representation in the lesbian movement. For this reason these authors in particular wish to stress that their article does not represent the opinion of all lesbians in Argentina, but is exclusively their point of view. They write about the situation of lesbians in a post-military regime, in particular about the group Las Lunas y Las Otras, a feminist lesbian group based in Buenos Aires, of which they are founder members.

None of the authors pretends to speak for all lesbians of their country. Nor do they all agree with each other. Each expresses exclusively their own understanding of the situation of lesbians and lesbian feminism in their country. That there are commonalities is often the result of years of collaborating and networking, as well as shared experiences of oppression. The Latin American contributors have worked together and exchanged experiences at Latin American and Caribbean Feminist and Lesbian *Encuentros*. Authors from Asia and the Pacific Islands are all members of the Asian Lesbian Network (ALN) founded in 1986, and have attended the network's conferences (Thailand 1990, Japan 1992, Taiwan 1995) to swap notes, exchange experiences, iron out (or respect) differences, and discuss and devise strategies. The African network is less formalized, and fewer open lesbian groups exist. As the African contributors argue, class and race barriers still undermine lesbian solidarity. FLOW is possibly the only open feminist lesbian group in Africa, but African lesbians are active in feminist groups and do work in lesbian and gay groups, as in Ghana, Zimbabwe, Namibia and the many groups that exist in South Africa.

The authors come from a variety of occupational backgrounds, a fact that is reflected in their writing styles, which range from the academic to the experiential. This was a deliberate decision, designed to present the diversity of lesbian lives. All would define themselves as lesbian feminist activists, which explains the emphasis on activism rather than theory in most of the contributions. The positions expressed range from a liberal defence and advocacy of lesbian human rights to attempts at a more radical analysis and call for a transformation of heteropatriarchy. All authors are aware of the limitations of their own location in their respective societies. This anthology is only offered as a beginning. Much research is necessary to fill the vacuum of information that exists about lesbians, in particular from rural areas, older lesbians and those whose oppression is compounded by disability, caste, class and race.

My own location as White, Western, able-bodied and educationally privileged has given me access to resources, contacts, countries and networks that enabled the commissioning of these articles. However, the difficulties I had anticipated in compiling contributions from countries spread all over the globe exceeded my expectations. Unreliable and slow postal services, disrupted fax and telephone lines, language barriers, the unavailability of computer disks or even computers, and e-mail restricted to the very few, turned communication into a somewhat nightmarish experience at times, making it difficult to meet publishers' deadlines. This was compounded by personal and political periods of crises as well as illness. However, the rewards were many. Most authors who were not friends already are now, and the vast file of accumulated communications includes much more than the material that relates specifically to this book. We communicated over issues such as campaigns, funding agencies, concrete experiences of discrimination, family, lovers and relationships. Given the lack of documentation of lesbian lives, many contributors found themselves in the position of pioneers, having to start their research from scratch, relying on private archives and people allowing them access to their lives and materials. This means that this book is much more than the work of the contributors and editor; it includes the efforts of many lesbians all over the world who have contributed their ideas, love and support.

NOTES

1. The terms 'White' and 'Black' are written in upper case to denote the social construction of 'race' within a system where White has been, and continues to be, constructed as superior to Black. In British anti-racist discourse the term Black has been used to signify commonalties among groups that have been subjected to British racism, past and present. More recently, the term is used to specifically refer to peoples of African descent, which is also the case within an international context. For a discussion of the inadequacy of terminology used to describe our 'racial' identities see Magdalene Ang-Lygate, 'Shades of meaning', *Trouble and Strife* 31 (1990 pp. 15–20).

2. Sharon Lim-Hing (ed.), *The Very Inside* (Toronto: Sister Vision Press, 1994). Valerie Mason-John (ed.) *Talking Black: Lesbians of African and Asian Descent Speak Out* (London: Cassell, 1995). Valerie Mason-John and Ann Khambatta *Lesbians Talk: Making Black Waves* (London: Scarlet Press, 1993). Juanita Ramos (ed.) *Compañeras: Latina Lesbians* (London: Routledge, 1994). Makeda Silvera (ed.) *Piece of My Heart: A Lesbian of Colour Anthology* (Toronto: Sister Vision Press, 1991). Carla Trujillo (ed.) *Chicana Lesbians: The Girls Our Mothers Warned Us About* (Berkeley: Third Woman Press, 1991).

3. Mark Gevisser and Edwin Cameron (eds) *Defiant Desire: Gay and Lesbian Lives in South Africa* (Johannesburg: Ravan Press, 1994). Matthew Krouse (ed.) *The Invisible Ghetto: Lesbian and Gay Writing from South Africa*

(Johannesburg: The Gay Men's Press, 1993). Tracy Moore (ed.) *Lesbiót: Israeli Lesbians Talk about Sexuality, Feminism, Judaism and their Lives* (London: Cassell, 1995).

4. *ILIS Newsletter* vol. 15, no. 2 (1994), p. 13.
5. *SISTER Namibia* vol. 7, no. 2 (1995), p. 31.
6. *Pink Paper*, 10 March 1995.
7. The last two terms were included in the regional *Platform for Action* drafted at the European and North American regional preparatory conference (Vienna 1994) for the Fourth United Nations World Conference on Women in Beijing, as a result of pressure from Arkadija, a lesbian group from Belgrade, who argued that many Eastern European lesbians do not identify as such.
8. *New Internationalist* (November 1989), special issue. 'Pride and prejudice: homosexuality', pp. 24–5.
9. *ILIS Newsletter* vol. 15, no. 3 (1994), p. 15.
10. 'Heteropatriarchy': a society based on and organized around heterosexual male domination.
11. Celia Kitzinger and Sue Wilkinson (eds), *Heterosexuality: A Feminism and Psychology Reader* (London: Sage, 1993), p. 31.
12. The term is derived from the Greek island of Lesbos, home of the famous poet Sappho (6th century BC) who loved women.
13. For a discussion of different forms of feminism see Maggie Humm (ed.) *Feminisms* (London: Harvester Wheatsheaf, 1992).
14. See for example: Sheila Jeffreys *Anticlimax* (London: The Women's Press, 1990). Celia Kitzinger *The Social Construction of Lesbianism* (London: Sage, 1987). Audre Lorde *A Burst of Light* (London: Sheba, 1988).
15. Elizabeth Khaxas and Liz Frank, 'Black sisters: Lesben', in F. Herve (ed.), *Namibia: Frauen mischen sich ein* (Berlin: Orlanda, 1993), pp. 107–9.
16. Cheryl Clarke 'The failure to transform: homophobia in the black community', in Barbara Smith (ed.), *Home Girls: A Black Feminist Anthology* (New York: Kitchen Table: Women of Color Press, 1983), pp. 197–208. Anne Hayfield *Shot by Both Sides* (London: Lesbian and Gay Employment Rights, 1995).

1 persecution and resistance

monika reinfelder

While the following articles focus on lesbian resistance, this chapter aims
to provide a brief overview of the global oppression of lesbians. In many
countries the legacy of colonialism/neo-colonialism and the effects of
continuing North/South inequalities have given priority to struggles
around poverty, illiteracy, famine and national liberation. This has often
rendered it impossible for women to engage in issues of sexuality. And
yet, lesbians are killed, raped, forced into arranged marriages, imprisoned,
submitted to psychiatric institutions, given electroconvulsive therapy or
medication to 'cure' them of their lesbianism, are driven into suicide,
excommunicated by their family, friends and communities, left without
food and drink in hospitals when ill, have no pension, inheritance,
housing and land rights, are deprived of custody of their children or
adoption rights, and are refused access to their partners due to discriminatory immigration and asylum legislation. The list is endless.

The most insidious oppression we face, however, is the denial of our
existence. Our invisibility is part of, and compounds, the heterosexism[1]
we are constantly subjected to, be it on an individual or institutional level.
It is, in fact, so powerful that we ourselves often believe we do not exist.
Even in the more 'liberal' countries, teenagers often grow up believing
they are the only ones who have these feelings. A British study revealed
that fourteen out of eighteen young lesbians had attempted to commit
suicide, many having tried to kill themselves a number of times.[2] This
isolation is exactly what the House of Lords (UK) had in mind when it
discussed possible punishment for lesbianism in 1921: death, incarceration in a 'lunatic asylum', or the third method, which they preferred: 'to
leave them entirely alone, not notice them, not advertise them. That is the
method that has been adopted in England for many hundred years, and I

believe that it is the best method now, these cases are self-exterminating.'[3]

In spite of lesbianism's self-exterminating 'qualities' UK Members of Parliament believed it to be the cause of 'the destruction of the early Greek civilisation, and still more the cause of the downfall of the Roman Empire'![4] Lesbianism had already escaped illegalization in 1885 when male homosexuality was recriminalized, allegedly because Queen Victoria did not believe such a phenomenon existed and could therefore not be legislated against. In true British colonial spirit these laws and attitudes were exported to countries Britain was in the process of destroying, notably India, which prior to colonization and religious fundamentalism had a rich history of diverse sexual behaviour (see Chapter three). As a result of the import of heterosexism the lesbian group Sakhi in New Delhi continues to receive letters from women in rural areas who believe suicide to be the only option to escape isolation and arranged marriage.[5] Anjaree, a lesbian group in Thailand, received ninety-four letters during one week from women who all had believed they were the only woman who loved other women until Anjaree's public appearance on TV and in a national newspaper. Invisibility, isolation, loneliness, being forced to lead a dishonest double life, or to restrict our lives and actions, are the most pernicious effects of discrimination against us. In the words of an Indonesian lesbian we are 'exiled into silence'.[6]

Given our supposed non-existence, fewer countries illegalize sexual relations between women than between men. Iran is the country with the worst record. Not only is lesbianism illegal, it also carries the death penalty. The execution methods are particularly cruel: hanging, stoning, being thrown off a cliff or high building, or facing a firing squad.[7] Amnesty International has received reports that some lesbians have been beheaded or stoned to death, but it has proved it extremely difficult to substantiate this.[8] Unconfirmed reports claim that in the early 1980s a number of lesbians and gay men were thrown off a cliff after they tried to form a lesbian and gay organization.[9] And on New Year's Day, 1990, two lesbians were stoned to death in the city of Langrood.[10] The following is an extract from the Bill of Retribution (*Quisas*), which was introduced by the Parliament of the Republic of Iran:

Article 127: *Mosaheqeh* [lesbianism] is the homosexuality of woman by genitals.

Article 128: The ways of proving lesbianism in court are the same by which the homosexuality (of men) is proved.

Article 129: The punishment for lesbianism is hundred (100) lashes for each party.

Article 130: Punishment for lesbianism will be established *vis-à-vis* someone who is mature, of sound mind, has free will and intention. Note: In the punishment for lesbianism there will be no distinction between the doer and the subject as well as a Muslim or non-Muslim.

Article 131: If the act of lesbianism is repeated three times and punishment is enforced each time, the death sentence will be issued the fourth time.

Article 132: If a lesbian repents before the giving of testimony by the witnesses, the punishment will be quashed; if she does so after the giving of testimony, the punishment will not be quashed.

Article 133: If the act of lesbianism is proved by the confession of the doer and she repents accordingly, the Sharia judge may request the leader (*Valie Amr*) to pardon her.

Article 134: If two women not related by consanguinity stand naked under one cover without necessity, they will be punished to less than hundred (100) lashes (*Ta'azir*). In case of its repetition as well as the repetition of punishment, hundred (100) lashes will be hit the third time.[11]

The proof requires four male witnesses. Needless to say that no Iranian lesbian was able to write an article for this anthology. Instead, an Iranian refugee living in Sweden comments on the situation of lesbians in Iran:

> Lesbians especially lead intolerable lives. Forced to marry through family pressure, those who show no interest in sexual relations are accused of failing to obey their husbands, which under Islam is grounds for divorce – often preceded by a long period of humiliation and beatings. Divorce brings even greater isolation and oppression; because the woman is no longer a virgin, her family believes she will misbehave sexually unless kept under constant supervision. Suspicions that she might be lesbian fuel their hostility.[12]

The situation of lesbians is generally dire in Middle Eastern countries. One lesbian living in this region replied to an invitation for a contribution to this anthology:

> The legal system in ... does not have a mention of the word *suhak* (lesbianism) ... lesbians are more than marginalized, they are non-existent in the main religion of the country. As a result, socially their existence is denied in the best part of the social structure. Lesbians in ... are without a mention, without recognition, very marginalized. Yet they exist. Their existence is limited to forming social groups that have no political form. The growing number of lesbians in the capital is evident in the past three years. ... There are different groups of lesbians. ... They come from different educational backgrounds and ages ... we will be associating and hopefully co-operating with our Palestinian and Israeli sisters ... to write up anything at this point is dangerous and early. [13]

During the United Nations International Conference on Population and Development in Cairo in 1994, several Middle Eastern and other Islamic countries objected to the rather ambiguous *Programme for Action* produced at the conference. The proposals do not address sexual orientation, but operate within a traditional definition of sexuality as heterosexual intercourse. Nevertheless, it caused concern during the conference. Fear was expressed that its references to 'individuals and couples' would undermine marriage, and its emphasis on sexual rights was seen as condoning lesbianism and homosexuality. While Islamic countries veiled their objections by vague references to Sharia law, other countries were more explicit: 'In Honduras these terms will never be able to mean unions of persons of the same sex. ... The government of Nicaragua ... also express[es] an explicit reservation on the term 'couples' and 'unions' when they may refer to persons of the same sex.'[14]

Post-Sandinista Nicaragua has became infamous for its new legislation on sexuality (among other things), which does not only include lesbians and gay men but anyone advocating lesbian and gay rights. Article 204 of the Penal Code came into force in 1992 and states that 'anyone who induces, promotes, propagandizes or practises in scandalous form sexual intercourse between persons of the same sex commits the crime of sodomy and shall incur 1 to 3 years' imprisonment'. Sodomy is defined as 'a sexual inversion, that is, anal copulation between two persons of the male sex or between two women [sic]' and as 'a deviation from normal life which subverts the foundations of a correct society, attached to ethical principles for the well-being of the family and the nation as a whole'. The practice of sodomy is seen as 'a threat to the holy institution of matrimony and procreation. ... To authorize its free practice would be a legal attack on the growth of the Nicaraguan population and a setback to its political, economic and social advancement.'[15] Herewith lesbians and gay men became a useful scapegoat for US aid to the Contras and the conservative Union Nacional Opositora government that undermined the referred to advancement of Nicaragua. In addition, if the Nicaraguan government had any training in the discipline of logic it would actually be forced to outlaw heterosexuality and its promotion, given that sodomy (penile penetration of the anus) is practised more by heterosexuals than by gay men and lesbians (a biological impossibility for the latter).[16]

Countries in which lesbianism is also a legal offence include Algeria, Burkina Faso, Ethiopia, Morocco, Tunisia, the Bahamas (20 year prison sentence), Trinidad and Tobago, Antigua and Barbuda, Barbados, Oman and Romania. Where lesbianism is not explicitly stated as a legal offence, as in the UK and a number of states in the USA, lesbians could never-theless be charged with public order offences such as 'breach of the peace', 'insulting behaviour' or 'indecent behaviour'. In Islamic countries, laws containing vague references to 'carnal knowledge against the order of nature' could be used against lesbians. This situation has led to the possibility that lesbians who are imprisoned because of their sexual orientation being adopted as 'prisoners of conscience' by Amnesty Inter-national.

In 1991 the human rights organization included persecution and impris-onment on the basis of sexual orientation in the definition of a prisoner of conscience, the result of a twelve-year campaigning effort by the Inter-national Lesbian and Gay Association (ILGA). However, so far no lesbian has been adopted as a prisoner of conscience. There are many reasons for this. First, not as many lesbians are imprisoned as gay men given that, as stated above, the definition of 'homosexual' is exclusively applied to men in many countries. Second, many lesbians are imprisoned for fictitious offences, as incarceration on the basis of sexual orientation would con-stitute an admission of the existence of lesbians. Therefore, as in the concentration camps in Nazi Germany where lesbians wore the black triangle of the 'anti-socials' (vagrants, petty criminals and prostitutes) rather than the pink triangle,[17] sexual orientation is not usually identified as the reason for the imprisonment of lesbians. Third, even if lesbianism is stated as the reason for imprisonment, an Amnesty International campaign to release the prisoner would probably only contribute to her oppression, as it would out her to what will most likely be a hostile world. This could mean excommunication or worse by her family, friends and community. It would also seriously undermine her chances in the labour market and therefore any possibility of an economically independent existence. It could lead to death threats, even her murder in the form of a family 'honour killing' or a death squad attempt at 'ethnic' or 'social cleansing'.

Thus is the 'fate' of many lesbians. The absence of capital punishment or legislation aimed at lesbians in some countries does not protect our lives. In some countries death squads are responsible for the deaths of many lesbians. Between 1986 and 1990 over 300 gay men and lesbians were killed in Colombia by death squads cleansing the country of 'antisocial elements'. Some of the victims displayed signs of torture or mutilation. In Brazil 1,200 gay men and lesbians were killed during the 1980s, again many of them at the hands of death squads. The perpetrators remain unpunished or receive very lenient sentences.[18] In the USA a study showed that one in ten lesbians had been punched, hit, kicked or beaten at least once in their lives because of their sexual orientation.[19] Two lesbians in Oregon were shot by their neighbour who took offence at their display of affection. Another 'offended' gunman killed one lesbian and wounded her lover when they were hiking in Pennsylvania.[20] Lesbians who set up Camp Sister Spirit (a training centre for women) in Mississippi constantly face violence and harassment by the local community. According to the New York City Gay and Lesbian Anti-Violence Project more than 150 lesbians and gay men were murdered in the USA between 1992 and 1994.[21] In Belgrade, two members of the lesbian group Arkadija were physically assaulted by men who recognized one of them after she had courageously come out on a TV programme.

It is, of course, impossible to determine the extent of violence against lesbians, be it public or in the home. In most cases a lesbian will refrain from reporting such crime. To identify her sexual orientation as the cause for the attack may well subject her to further abuse. Or she will risk being outed, with possible disastrous consequences on her family life and/or employment. This is doubly the case for Black women and women of colour who live in White racist societies and are therefore dependent on their families' and communities' support. Lesbians in prison are also particularly vulnerable, especially if they experience violence or torture, and often face further discrimination, as they may not be able to make use of the legal, social or counselling services available to other prisoners. They may also face harsher sentences, as the judges and jurors often regard their sexual orientation as 'proof' of culpability.

Other forms of violence are inflicted on lesbians, notably by the medical profession. In many countries lesbians receive psychiatric treatment to 'cure' them of their lesbianism. In the UK a study of lesbian and gay teenagers showed that one out of seven young lesbians and gay men had been sent to a psychiatrist.[22] Until the 1950s hysterectomies, hormone injections and clitoridectomies[23] were performed on lesbians in the USA, practices that only stopped when Dr Evelyn Hooker 'proved' that homosexuality was not an illness. This also applies to electroconvulsive therapy, which was forced on lesbians in the USA and Western Europe, and is still used as a 'treatment' in many countries, for example Russia, Romania, Mexico and China. In the UK many lesbians have reported the use of this treatment for depression. No counselling had been offered that identified their oppression as lesbians as the cause for their depression. Therapists still often view lesbianism as a sexual perversion/illness at worst and as 'arrested development' at best. This is the case in spite of the World Health Organization having removed homosexuality from its list of illnesses in 1993. The American Psychiatric Association had made a similar move twenty years earlier when it declassified homosexuality as a pathology (although individual psychiatrists do not necessarily abide by this). The psychiatric profession in other countries obviously have not followed suit. For example, the lesbian group Arkadija in Belgrade was forced out of their housing, which they shared with other NGOs, after a group of psychiatrists claimed that it was 'unethical' for lesbians to help women survivors of war crimes.

In spite of the level of persecution described above, discrimination on the basis of sexual orientation has not yet made its way into the formal definition of a refugee. The 1951 Geneva Convention on Refugees defines a refugee as a person who is persecuted on the basis of race, religion, nationality, membership of a particular social group or for holding a particular political opinion. Campaigners have argued that lesbians and gay men constitute a 'particular social group', and should therefore be included in the definition. A similar argument, in a different context, was presented by the European Parliament in 1984. Its resolution recommended to member states the inclusion of women who have been subjected to domestic violence, and continue to be under the threat of violence, in the definition of a 'particular social group'. Both recommendations continue to be rejected.

However, some countries have granted discretionary refugee status to women fleeing male violence, as well as to those escaping persecution on the basis of sexual orientation. Canada has offered asylum to women who in their country were subjected to male violence; the government is adamant, however, that this was discretionary and does not set a precedent. Together with the USA, Australia, the Scandinavian countries, the

Netherlands, Austria and the UK, Canada has also granted asylum for persecution on the basis of sexual orientation. Germany set an example in 1990 by granting asylum to an Iranian lesbian who would have faced the death penalty had she been forced to return to Iran. A few years later a Russian lesbian applied for refugee status, claiming that on her return to Russia she would be incarcerated in a psychiatric hospital. Although it is well known that this is the fate of lesbians, not only in Russia but also in other countries, notably Romania, China and Mexico, it is very difficult to prove, as no documentation exists. Many governments interpret vaguely worded legislation (e.g. 'sexual act against nature') as only applying to men, not recognizing that they provide repressive contexts within which violations against lesbians are commonplace. This, as well as the hatred of lesbians in most countries, has prevented many persecuted lesbians from applying for refugee status on the basis of their sexual orientation. Instead they predominantly claim political persecution, albeit not always successfully. In 1994 the Immigration Appeal Tribunal in the UK set a precedent by ruling that lesbians and gay men facing persecution in their country *may* qualify as members of a particular social group in line with the 1951 Refugee Convention.

Lesbians may of course want to change their country of residence for reasons other than persecution. Some want to join their partners, but many lesbian couples are split up due to discriminatory legislation that does not grant immigration rights to same-sex couples. In Europe and North America this is compounded by racist immigration legislation. This leads to the paradoxical situation of some lesbian feminists supporting campaigns for same-sex marriage. While all lesbian feminists are in favour of partnership rights for lesbians, few would normally support such a blatantly heteropatriarchal institution. However, given the lack of immigration rights for same-sex partners in most countries, the possibility of marriage is seen as the only chance for lesbian couples to stay together. At the moment lesbians without residence rights still have to adopt the risky and often expensive façade of a heterosexual marriage to be able to stay with their partners. Some couples become permanent travellers, moving from one country to the next every time their visas expire. Of course, this has a detrimental effect on their work and financial situation, as well as often putting a strain on the relationship. A non-European lesbian ended up in prison for three months in Germany when immigration officials checked her expired visa at the airport just as she was about to leave the country with her German partner. The few countries that have immigration rights for same-sex couples are Australia, Aoteoroa/New Zealand, Canada,

South Africa, the Netherlands, Norway, Sweden, Denmark, Finland and Spain. Civil marriage is possible in Denmark, Sweden and Norway.

Lesbian feminists are aware of the limitation of rights legislation to combat oppression. However, many lesbians are beginning to use international human rights mechanisms for their own ends. Following the Women's Rights are Human Rights campaign initiated by the Global Centre for Women's Leadership, lesbian groups in many countries now look to international human rights instruments for support. They predominantly base their claim to human rights protection on Article 2 of the Universal Declaration of Human Rights (UDHR), which recognizes the 'inherent dignity and . . . the equal and inalienable rights of all members of the human family', and guarantees the protection of the fundamental rights and freedom of all people, 'without distinction of any kind, such as race, colour, sex, language . . . or other status'.

Much of international human rights law emerged in reaction to the atrocities committed during the Second World War. And yet, although lesbians were a persecuted group in Nazi Germany,[24] they are excluded from international human rights protection. Human rights concepts and institutions are male-defined, and the existing human rights discourse requires evidence of the reality of the problem in the form of statistics and hard data. The invisibility of lesbians and the even greater invisibility of the abuse of lesbians makes it difficult to prove such violations of our human rights. The torture of a man in prison is more easily detected than the torture of a lesbian who suffers daily rape in a forced marriage. Prolonged solitary confinement in prison is internationally recognized as a form of torture. Social isolation of lesbians is not. Nor is the enforcement of heterosexuality.[25]

However, governments are obliged to protect the lives of their citizens (at least in theory). If they fail to do so they are in breach of international law. Although an act of violence on the part of a private individual is not covered by international legislation, the failure of a government to protect individuals against such acts or to punish the perpetrators constitutes a violation of international law. There have indeed been cases where international human rights legislation has overridden domestic discriminative laws on sexual orientation (e.g. in the UK, Ireland and Cyprus). However, many countries, notably Nicaragua, will fall back on the security of a cultural moral relativism that 'protects' their country from progressive human rights legislation or recommendations. Custom always becomes sacred and unchangeable as soon as women want to bring about change for their own benefit. But, as expressed by the former Chief Justice of the

Supreme Court of India, 'universal human rights standards are rooted in all cultures, religions and traditions, but those cultural, religious and traditional practices that undermine universality and prove harmful to women cannot be tolerated.'[26]

Some efforts have been made by individual countries to introduce anti-discrimination laws that make it illegal to discriminate on the basis of sexual orientation: for example, in Denmark, Sweden, Norway, the Netherlands, France, Ireland, Germany (state of Brandenburg), Aoteoroa/New Zealand, Australia, Israel, Namibia, Brazil, some states in the USA, and Canada (Quebec, Ontario). The European Parliament passed a resolution in 1994 that calls on member states to end discrimination based on sexual orientation. Claudia Roth (a member of the German Green Party), who introduced the resolution, has since been excommunicated by the Pope; and her parents, who live in Germany's deep south, have been sent numerous copies of the Bible!

Another attempt to address human rights abuses of lesbians involved the active participation of lesbians from all over the world at the Fourth United Nations World Conference on Women in Beijing (WCW), and the numerous preparatory meetings that took place prior to the conference in many countries and regions.

Lesbians in Beijing

In spite of calls for a boycott due to China's poor human rights record,[27] Latin American, African, Asian and Pacific Islander lesbians campaigned to put lesbian issues on the agenda of the WCW. Unlike many lesbian feminists in Western Europe and the USA who do not wish to be involved in United Nations politics, or who attended the conference as members of NGOs (non-governmental organizations) concerned with issues other than lesbian oppression, many Latin American, African, Asian and Pacific Islander lesbians were present as lesbians, fighting for lesbian issues. Much time had already been taken up, both at the Latin American and Caribbean Lesbian Feminist *Encuentro* in Argentina (April 1995) and during Asian Lesbian Network (ALN) meetings, by discussions that focused on Beijing. Many participants withdrew from the preparations; but others had already attended the regional preparatory conferences for Beijing in Jakarta and in Buenos Aires, during which important lessons were to be learned, in particular during meetings preceding the preparatory conferences.

The ALN and its supporters had prepared a resolution during an Asia/Pacific meeting of NGOs in Manila which received much applause from conference participants. The resolution demanded

> that discrimination against lesbians be documented; that references to lesbians not be removed from preparatory documents and that these documents and resolutions not marginalize lesbians; that there be recognition of the right of women to choose lifestyles and partners without discrimination; that the violence against lesbians perpetuated by homophobia and sanctioned by state, religion and culture be condemned and stopped; and that the treatment of women's issues not silence individual women who choose not to marry and not to live with a male partner.[28]

However, by the following meeting in Bangkok all references to lesbians had been edited out, and microphones were switched off when attempts were made to address lesbian issues.

Latin American lesbians were better prepared for the regional preparatory conference in Buenos Aires. They had organized a prior meeting in Lima to design strategies, and lesbian groups from ten countries participated. During the last pre-Beijing meeting of NGOs in New York Patria Jimenez from the group El Closet de Sor Juana (Mexico) delivered a speech to the United Nations Commission on the Status of Women on behalf of the Lesbian Caucus demanding the inclusion of sexual orientation in the final draft of the *Platform for Action*.

> Madam Chairwoman
>
> It is a very great honour to have this opportunity to address the Commission on the Status of Women on the occasion of this preparatory meeting for the Fourth World Conference on Women. I speak as a representative of the Lesbian Caucus, which includes women from Sri Lanka, Ecuador, the United States, Malaysia, the Netherlands, Costa Rica, Barbados, Canada, and several other countries.
>
> The Fourth World Conference on Women presents us with a historic opportunity. We have come a great distance in the twenty years since the First World Conference on Women. In 1993, at the World Conference on Human Rights, the governments of the world recognized that women's rights are inalienable, indivisible, and universal human rights. Yet lesbians continue to experience a wide range of human rights abuses, including imprisonment and murder, forced psychiatric confinement, verbal harassment, physical violence, and discrimination in employment, education, social benefits

programmes, housing and health care. In the face of these and many other abuses of our human rights, the draft *Platform for Action* contains not a single mention of sexual orientation, and it is this omission that we ask you, the assembled delegates, to remedy in this preparatory meeting.

We in the Latin American and Caribbean region have been active participants since the advent of the preparations for the Beijing conference, as have lesbians in Asia and the Pacific, Africa, Europe and North America. We have worked within the national and regional preparations, as we are now working within this final preparatory meeting, for recognition of our human rights. We have met with a broad consensus of support among the many NGOs that are active in these preparations. Yet we find no reflection of this support in the *Platform for Action*, a crucial document that will determine our social and political participation in the decade to come.

We must remember that one of the central themes of this historic conference is the inclusion of NGOs in the decisions that will guide future actions and programmes to secure a world of equality, development, and peace. I have here the signatures of more than six thousand people from over sixty countries representing every region of the world. These individuals, along with over 150 organizations – women's groups, human rights groups, groups concerned with development and with health care – have called on you, the Member States, to recognize the right to determine one's sexual identity; the right to control one's own body, particularly in establishing intimate relationships; and the right to choose if, when, and with whom to bear children as fundamental components of the human rights of all women regardless of sexual orientation.

The Fourth World Conference on Women presents us with the opportunity to bring to fruition that which is proclaimed in the Universal Declaration of Human Rights, which recognizes the 'inherent dignity and . . . the equal and inalienable rights of all members of the human family', and guarantees the protection of the fundamental rights and freedom of all people 'without distinction of any kind, such as race, colour, sex, language . . . or other status' (Article 2).

In so doing, we can take as inspiration the historic recognition last year by the UN Committee on Human Rights that sexual orientation is included in the Universal Declaration's guarantee of universal, indivisible, and inalienable human rights for all people. We can also take as examples the anti-discrimination laws in Australia, Brazil, Israel, Canada, and several other countries. And above all we can find inspiration in the Constitution of the new South Africa, which prohibits discrimination on the basis of sexual orientation.

If it is true that the Fourth World Conference on Women speaks in the name of all of the world's women, in all of their complex and multiple diversity, it must also speak in our name. The equality of the rights of citizenship is a fundamental aim of democracy, a goal to which all of us aspire. True equality, however, will never exist until we begin to truly respect the right to difference.

Many countries showed support; others, notably the Vatican, did not. As a result the draft *Platform for Action* included sexual orientation, albeit in brackets. This signified that it required further discussion to prevent its exclusion from the final *Platform for Action*[29] at the Beijing conference.

In spite of these shortcomings lesbians were much more prepared for this conference than they had been for previous ones. A few courageous lesbians discussed issues of sexuality at the First United Nations WCW in Mexico in 1975, which marked the beginning of the United Nations Decade for Women. And there were still attempts to exclude lesbians at the third conference held in Nairobi in 1985. The International Lesbian Information Service (ILIS) organized press conferences to raise awareness about lesbians, in particular about those from non-Western countries who claimed to be sick and tired of being told that they had caught a Western disease. During a workshop on lesbians and employment we were told by a member of the African National Congress (ANC) that homosexuality is a Western disease brought to South Africa through imperialism. A public (heart-warming) apology was subsequently offered by another ANC member in London: 'I . . . regret deeply the hurt and the sense of rejection from an ANC speaker at the Nairobi Conference regarding the struggle by lesbians against oppression. . . . ANC women support lesbian women, for our struggle *is* the same. Please accept this apology.'[30]

In Beijing the South African government fully supported the inclusion of sexual orientation in the *Platform for Action*. At the NGO Forum, for the first time in the history of the United Nations Women's Conferences, lesbians had their own space (the lesbian tent) within which to hold workshops, meet, network, devise strategies and organize campaigns. Activities in the tent gave new impetus to the recently formed African lesbian network and initial attempts were made to form an East and West European lesbian network. ILIS and the International Gay and Lesbian Human Rights Commission (IGLHRC) produced global human rights reports on lesbians;[31] and they also distributed information about lesbianism in Chinese, which was confiscated by the Chinese authorities, but further copies generated much interest and support from Chinese women.

As did a lesbian 'parade' (demonstrations were illegal) that attracted over 500 women as well as the media. Daphne Scholinski's (USA) testimony of her incarceration in a psychiatric hospital, diagnosed as suffering from a 'gender identity disorder' (the treatment of which included the imposition of masculine-identified femininity), received a standing ovation during the Global Tribunal on Accountability for Women's Human Rights.

At the main conference the Lesbian Caucus (with members from all regions) worked hard to ensure the inclusion of sexual orientation in the *Platform for Action*. Most governmental delegations were lobbied, and Beverley Ditsie (South Africa) gave an impassioned speech that caused much media attention:

> Madam Chair
>
> It is a great honour to have the opportunity to address this distinguished body on behalf of the International Gay and Lesbian Human Rights Commission, the International Lesbian Information Service, the International Lesbian and Gay Association, and over fifty other organizations. My name is Palesa Beverley Ditsie and I am from Soweto, South Africa, where I have lived all my life and experienced both tremendous joy and pain within my community.
>
> I come from a country that has recently had an opportunity to start afresh, an opportunity to strive for a true democracy where the people govern and where emphasis is placed on the human rights of all people. The Constitution of South Africa prohibits discrimination on the basis of race, gender, ethnic or social origin, colour, sexual orientation, age, disability, religion, conscience, belief, culture, or language. In his opening parliamentary speech in Cape Town on the 9th of April 1994, His Excellency Nelson Rolihlahla Mandela, State President of South Africa, received resounding applause when he declared that never again would anyone be discriminated against on the basis of sexual orientation.
>
> The Universal Declaration of Human Rights recognizes the 'inherent dignity and ... the equal and inalienable rights of all members of the human family', and guarantees the protection of the fundamental rights and freedoms of all poeple 'without distinction of any kind, such as race, colour, sex, language ... or other status' (Article 2). Yet every day, in countries around the world, lesbians suffer violence, harassment and discrimination because of their sexual orientation. Their basic human rights – such as the right to life, to bodily integrity, to freedom of association and expression – are violated. Women who love women are fired from their jobs; forced into marriages; beaten and murdered in their homes and on the streets; and have their

children taken away by hostile courts. Some commit suicide due to the isolation and stigma that they experience within their families, religious institutions and their broader community. These and other abuses are documented in a recently released report by the International Gay and Lesbian Human Rights Commission on sexual orientation and women's human rights, as well as in reports by Amnesty International. Yet the majority of these abuses have been difficult to document because although lesbians exist everywhere in the world (including Africa), we have been marginalized and silenced and remain invisible in most of the world.

In 1994, the United Nations Human Rights Committee declared that discrimination based on sexual orientation violates the right to non-discrimination and the right to privacy guaranteed in the International Covenant of Civil and Political Rights. Several countries have passed legislation prohibiting discrimination based on sexual orientation. If the World Conference on Women is to address the concerns of *all* women, it must similarly recognize that discrimination based on sexual orientation is a violation of basic human rights. Paragraphs 48 and 226 of the *Platform for Action* recognize that women face particular barriers in their lives because of many factors, including sexual orientation. However, the term 'sexual orientation' is currently in brackets. If these words are omitted from the relevant paragraphs, the *Platform for Action* will stand as one more symbol of the discrimination that lesbians face, and of the lack of recognition of our very existence.

No woman can determine the direction of her own life without the ability to determine her sexuality. Sexuality is an integral, deeply ingrained part of every human being's life and should not be subject to debate or coercion. Anyone who is truly committed to women's human rights must recognize that every woman has the right to determine her sexuality free of discrimination and oppression.

I urge you to make this a conference for *all* women, regardless of their sexual orientation, and to recognize in the *Platform for Action* that lesbian rights are women's rights and that women's rights are universal, inalienable, and indivisible human rights. I urge you to remove the brackets from sexual orientation. Thank you.

At 4.30 a.m. on the last day of the conference 'sexual orientation' was deleted from the *Platform for Action*. However, members of the Lesbian Caucus claimed success. Pleased with the intensity, the length and the seriousness of the debate their press release was optimistic: 'The closet doors have swung open wide at the FWCW'. It was the first time that the issue of persecution based on sexual orientation had been deliberated at a United Nations conference, and lesbians (wearing a 'lesbian rights are human rights' badge) were numerous and visible at the proceedings. More than forty countries indicated that they would interpret the *Platform for Action* as prohibiting discrimination on the basis of sexual orientation as it prohibits discrimination on the grounds of 'other status'. In addition, one important clause remains in the text:

> The human rights of women include their right to have control over and decide fully and responsibly on matters relating to their sexuality, including sexual and reproductive health, free of coersion, discrimination and violence.

This is the most radical statement on sexuality ever to be included in a UN document. The *Platform for Action* itself is not legally binding, but as an agreement that can be used for campaigning purposes it does pave the way for a more explicit protection of lesbian rights on an international level.

In Beijing, as elsewhere, it was noticeable how even lesbians are often stunned at the extent of oppression experienced by other lesbians all over the world. This chapter is intended as a brief overview of such abuse, which, for some, proved too much to bear. They are no longer with us and we miss them. Some give in to compulsory heterosexuality; for others a change to heterosexuality is perceived as desirable, but an impossibility. Fortunately, for many of us our lesbianism is a conscious 'choice', albeit one that the institution of heterosexuality structures and constrains.[32] But in spite of the extreme difficulties and constraints this 'choice' may impose on us, we like and *prefer* being lesbians. We prefer our more exciting and interesting lifestyles, our politics, our friendships, our emotional and sexual relationships, even if they are difficult at times. As the British comedienne Hufty replied to the Church's contention that it is OK to be homosexual as long as we don't practise it: 'I don't need to practise, I'm good at it already!' Why change something we are good at?

NOTES

1. 'Heterosexism': the institutionalized belief that heterosexuality is the only form of sexual expression, or at least is superior to homosexuality. The term was introduced by Charlotte Bunch in 1976.

2. Jane Bridget 'Perspectives on lesbians' and gays' mental health', in *Directory of Lesbian and Gay Studies in the* UK (London: DOLAGS, 1993).

3. Sheila Jeffreys *The Spinster and Her Enemies: Feminism and Sexuality 1930–1980* (London: Pandora, 1985), p. 114.

4. *Ibid.*

5. Giti Thadani, interview with BBC Radio 5, 23 July 1995.

6. BJD Gayatri 'Coming out but remaining hidden: a portrait of lesbians in Java', Thirteenth International Congress on Anthropological and Ethnological Sciences in Mexico City, July 1993, conference paper to be published, p. 18. See also: Dawn Snape, Katarina Thomson and Mark Chetwynd *Discriminating Against Gay Men and Lesbians: A Study of the Nature and Extent of Discrimination Against Homosexual Men and Women in Britain Today* (London: Social and Community Planning Research, 1995).

7. *Human Rights for All: A Global View of Lesbian and Gay Oppression and Liberation* (Reading: Reading International Support Centre, 1992).

8. Amnesty International USA *Breaking the Silence: Human Rights Violations Based on Sexual Orientation* (New York: Amnesty International Publications, 1994).

9. Rex Wockner, 'Iran executes gays'. *Outlines*, March 1991.

10. Rex Wockner, 'Iran begins gay and lesbian genocide'. *Outlines*, March 1990.

11. Communication from Tehran Law Offices to the International Gay and Lesbian Human Rights Commission (IGLHRC), 1992.

12. *Human Rights for All*, p. 33.

13. Letter to the editor, 26 March 1995. The name of the country is deleted to protect anonymity.

14. United Nations, *International Conference on Population and Development: Programme of Action* (New York: UN, 1994), pp. 138–9. For an evaluation of the Cairo conference and an analysis of the relationship between heterosexuality and women's reproductive (ill) health, see Eva Gamarnikow and Monika Reinfelder 'In the name of tradition: human rights abuses of women', in J. Lynch, S. Modgil and C. Modgil *Education and Development: Tradition and Innovation – Equity and Excellence in Education for Development* (London: Cassell, forthcoming).

15. *Nicaragua Article 204: Legalizing the Repression of Homosexuality* (London: Amnesty International 1994), pp. 1,3.

16. 'Pride and prejudice: homosexuality', *New Internationalist* (November 1989), special issue.

17. The pink triangle had to be worn by gay men in Nazi concentration camps to identify them as homosexuals. Today the pink and black triangles are reclaimed by gay men and lesbians respectively, who wear them with pride. See Heinz Heger *The Men with the Pink Triangle* (London: GMP Publishers, 1980, first published in German in 1972).
18. *Zeitschrift der Informationsstelle Lateinamerika* nr 165 (1993) p.15.
19. ILIS *Newsletter* vol. 15, no. 2 (1994).
20. Gregory M. Herek and Kevin T. Berrill (eds.) *Hate Crimes: Confronting Violence Against Lesbians and Gay Men* (London: Sage, 1992).
21. *Pink Paper*, 17 February 1995.
22. Lorraine Trenchard and Hugh Warren *Something To Tell You* (London: London Gay Teenage Group, 1984).
23. Kathleen Barry sees the clitoridectomies that are performed on millions of women today as an attempt at the excision of autonomous female sexuality: *Female Sexual Slavery* (Englewood Cliffs, NJ: Prentice-Hall, 1979).
24. Gunter Grau (ed.), *Hidden Holocaust: Gay and Lesbian Persecution in Germany 1933–45* (London: Cassell, 1995). Claudia Schoppmann *Nationalsozialistische Sexualpolitik und Weibliche Homosexualitat* (Pfaffenweiler: Centaurus-Verlagsgesellschaft, 1991).
25. Forced heterosexuality or 'compulsory heterosexuality' was named as a crime against women at the International Tribunal on Crimes Against Women in Brussels, 1976. It was also identified as a human rights violation at the Global Tribunal on Violations of Women's Human Rights, United Nations World Conference on Human Rights in Vienna, 1993. The term 'compulsory heterosexuality' is usually associated with Adrienne Rich, *Compulsory Heterosexuality and Lesbian Existence* (London: Onlywomen Press, 1981). However, the institution of heterosexuality was already identified as a cornerstone of male supremacy by Charlotte Bunch in 1975. For a critique of the liberal connotation of the concept of compulsory heterosexuality, see Sheila Jeffreys *Anticlimax* (London: The Women's Press, 1990).
26. Justice P. N. Bhagwati, speaking at the Global Tribunal on Violation of Women's Human Rights. The tribunal in Vienna included the testimony of the Secretary General of the International Lesbian and Gay Association (ILGA), Rebecca Sevilla from Peru.
27. See Ann Khambatta, 'Legitimating repression: China and the UN Fourth World Conference on Women', *National Women's Network Newsletter* (July 1995) pp. 4–5.
28. ILIS *Newsletter* vol. 15, no. 2 (1994), pp. 8–9.

29. The *Platform for Action* is the final document of the conference, including a series of recommendations which, however, place no legal obligation on individual governments.

30. Post-Nairobi Women's Conference, Hackney, London, 1984. The borough of Hackney allegedly has the highest (out) lesbian population in Europe.

31. Shelly Anderson (ed.), *Lesbian Rights are Human Rights!* (Amsterdam: International Lesbian Information Service, 1995).
Rachel Rosenbloom (ed.), *Unspoken Rules: Sexual Orientation and Women's Human Rights* (San Francisco: International Gay and Lesbian Human Rights Commission, 1995).

32. For a succinct critique of the concept of 'choice' applied to sexuality, see: Yvon Appleby 'Heterosexuality: compulsion, choice or a strong pair of arms?', *Feminism and Psychology* vol. 5, no. 1 (February 1995) pp. 136–9.

2 stolen strands: the in and out lives of lesbians in the philippines

malu marin

orange thread in woof
and purple thread in warp
mingle mindlessly;
snag;
and discover
they become each other,

embracing tightly for sturdiness,
lightly for smoothness,
stretching out days
mending lapses in lacing,
stretching out nights
embroidering dreams,

finding reasons
for lingering
without entangling,
making extra knits
to justify
a purple and orange loom

to spin
whatever web,
to weave
whatever joy
out of thin and stolen strands.

Taken from 'Weaving' by A. L. Sarabia (1982)

A not-too distant past

The pursuit of the past is a project preserved for the purposeful, the persistent and the persevering. And when the past, just like the present, is construed to be non-existent and invisible, when no 'hard facts' or data are on hand to give evidence to a previous existence, determining when and how things or circumstances come into being, it becomes a tedious and painstaking process. Establishing the possibility of a precursor or historical precedent becomes all the more urgent, a task necessary in order to comprehend present phenomena and to arrive at an understanding of how its historical existence impacts on its present state. The current research efforts on Philippine lesbian history are faced with a serious dilemma: there is no record or known historical document that provides evidence of lesbian historical existence; but there is none that disproves it either. The silence of history on lesbianism is loud and clear.

What is most required then, from diggers of the past, is the unflinching conviction that at some point in history there were lesbians in the Philippines who lived and loved, who either had to conform to the rigid norms and mores of their society or rebel and break the rules of that conformity. Women chieftains and warriors, the *Babaylans* or spiritual healers, daughters of powerful *datus*, women hunters and fishers, those without children and male relations: some of them may have chosen to live autonomously from men and may have chosen to love women. In secret and silence, or with an openness that may have shocked their society, lesbians must have exercised their rights to their sexuality. These are but mere hypotheses, however, that must be answered in a more in-depth and comprehensive study and re-examination of the past.

In the Philippines, there has been no attempt to achieve a level of scholarship that traces the roots of lesbianism to its historical beginnings. Anthropologists state in concert that there is no known study of lesbians in Philippine indigenous cultures and communities.[1] Some anthropologists, however, hold the opinion that lesbianism and homosexuality may have been normal, commonplace practices during the early times.[2] And precisely because it was accepted as a cultural practice and way of life that exhibited no 'remarkable' characteristics, it did not merit any form of documentation. Lesbian and homosexual practices were then present and these were taken as part of the cultural experience of the indigenous tribes and settlers. This rationalization for historical silence might in fact reveal that the chroniclers did not want to record anything so 'ordinary'.

Researchers may have imposed an understanding of lesbianism or homosexuality that was based on their understanding of it from their own cultural milieux. Its manifestation in the cultures of the peoples they are 'studying' however, might be very different, and may occur in forms they are unable to recognize. It is also the case that the homophobic biases of researchers could also come into play.

On the other hand, a number of Filipino anthropologists hold the view that because of the rigidity of gender roles in some tribal societies, any deviation commands immediate notice. Thus, the specificity of women's roles *vis-à-vis* the male roles makes it easy to discern what constitutes conformist or non-conformist behaviour. Thus, to interpret a man's interest and proficiency in doing beadwork or basketry as indicative of homosexual behaviour would be subject to contention. Gender-specific skills and activities varied from community to community, and it would be equally risky to draw the same conclusions with women who become historically noted for their physical prowess or strength, an area long reserved for men. It is also safe to assume that the reason why men or women cross over certain boundaries of gender-specific roles may have little to do with their sexual orientation.

The past is not too distant because there is no factual or evidential past to speak of. The past we can speak of then, may be a reconstructed past, made through glimpses of dark historical tunnels. We must then take into consideration the biases and prejudices of that period – and these are determined not from what the chroniclers have reported on, but from what they may have consciously omitted or excluded from their accounts.

Researchers of lesbian history face the daunting task of perusing and examining existing documents and texts, and in most cases are discouraged by dismissals from so-called experts on anthropology, history, sociology, politics and other related fields. The task of reconstruction remains to be done, and lesbian researchers will no doubt take longer to unravel their memories and buried past.

Unearthing lesbian history: in search of clues

The Spanish fleet first landed on Philippine shores in 1521. Although this attempt to set foot was not successful, it did not stop the Spanish monarchy from entering into agreements with other European navigators and explorers, not only to search for gold and spices in the Orient but also to spread Christianity. In the years 1565–71, the Conquistador Miguel

Lopez de Legaspi, accompanied by six Augustinian priests, helped Spain to establish its colony in the Philippines and so begin Spanish rule. For the next 370 years, the Philippines, especially its women, existed in a climate of economic dependence and political and intellectual repression. The Roman Catholic religion was preached and used by the Spaniards to legitimize their colonization of the Philippines. Indeed, it is said that the Christian cross succeeded in subjugating the indigenous ancestors more successfully than did the sword. The cross continues to shine above people's lives today, often blinding them instead of giving light.

While there are no actual historical documents or accounts that refer to lesbian cultures or experiences in pre-Hispanic and Hispanic society, certain archival documents containing references to lesbian existence may yet be unearthed and examined. The religious archives, such as the friar accounts and the confessionals which contained information on the 'moral situation' of the Filipino converts, surely reflect views on sexuality as perceived by the religious chroniclers.[3] The confessionals in particular, packaged as questions answerable with a yes or a no, are an adaptation of the ten commandments, designed to facilitate confession. Information on the 'sins' of the populace are recorded in these documents. Given the political and cultural context of Europe in the sixteenth and seventeenth centuries, it is not surprising that similar moral codes were enforced in the islands. Homosexuality and lesbianism may have qualified as violations of these moral codes.

Aside from looking for lesbianism in the religious context, the political situation, which had been documented both by friars and state rulers as well as the emerging Filipino intellectuals, may also contain such references. In particular, the accounts of the revolts and the Philippine revolution contain descriptions of women fighters and revolutionary soldiers, some of whom may have been lesbians.

It must be noted that there has been no attempt to reread and reinterpret historical texts and documents. The invisibility of lesbian existence in both past and contemporary Philippine society, in written texts and celluloid images, in academic discourse and liberation struggles has roots as deep as the Pacific waters. Unless phenomena involving women was outstanding, the chroniclers of pre-Hispanic and Hispanic Philippines generally excluded women from their accounts. For instance, in describing women's intellectual status in sixteenth-century Philippines, one priest-historian wrote, 'There was hardly a man, much less a woman, who could not read or write.' At a time when texts are being reread and reinterpreted, women's contributions and roles have assumed major importance. Because gender is now looked at as a category, more and more data and information have been gathered and collated. Texts are now being reinterpreted and re-examined in the light of their gender component.

The dearth of recorded empirical data on lesbianism has made researchers become critical and flexible in their research methods. The best sources of information are first person accounts and interviews with lesbians, and with feminists from disciplines such as sociology, anthropology and history. Moreover, one has to sharpen one's senses and be acutely aware of clues or cues, where references are made to lesbians without the actual mention of the 'L' word.

Lesbians in contemporary society: a socio-cultural context

In any society that operates within rigidly stratified sex and gender roles, any departure or digression from such stratification would not go unnoticed or unchecked. The entire community functions as a conscious and unconscious harmonizer. A conscious harmonizer is manifested concretely by directly confronting behaviour or actions that run counter to community mores and practices. Thus, it is not unusual for a lesbian or a gay man to be reprimanded by strangers in public places such as markets, streets or neighbourhood centres.[4] Unconscious harmonizers function in the unspoken and unwritten codes of any society. The manner of dressing, of walking, of simply doing things: all these have sex and gender-role implications which may not be verbally articulated, but nevertheless contain 'police' powers that are enough to keep individuals in their place.

Furthermore, rural and urban contexts invariably mould and shape the circumstances in which lesbian existence may evolve. In the rural areas, the interaction and interrelationships of people are more defined and structured. Thus, community norms and 'rules' exert more control over people. Also, because of the smallness of the community, blood relations are extended and the family has been redefined to include relations of consanguinity from the fourth or fifth degree. Thus the extended nature of family relations facilitates the regulation of behaviour in consonance with established community or familial norms and patterns.[5] It also becomes a perfect justification to 'convince' or compel individuals to conform to these norms. Any contrary behaviour is interpreted as an act of bringing disgrace and shame to the family. Lesbianism and homosexuality belong to such categories that defame or smear a person's or family's good moral standing. It is not unlikely, therefore, that lesbians and gay men migrate to urban centres for solace and space. Most lesbians describe how they are able to lead freer lives when they do not have direct contact and inter-action with their family. Not only can they express themselves more openly, they are able to pursue jobs and career opportunities which would not be available to them otherwise.

Urban centres also cater to varied forms of lifestyles. The realities of urban existence are starkly different from life in the rural areas. While it is true that in both urban and rural contexts resources are scarce for the majority and economic survival looms as the single most important concern, the stress and rigours are much more keenly felt by urban-based peoples. Life in urban centres is fast-paced and consumption-dependent, and in view of its inherent complexities, such an existence would tend to accommodate a continuum of lifestyles befitting urban survival: popula-tion is denser and family arrangements become more diverse. The range of acceptable behaviour in these areas is forever widening, and this is enough to attract people whose lives run counter to mainstream mores and norms. Much can be said about the impetus for these changes. In the recent decades, changes in the economic, political, and cultural spheres have brought about parallel changes in lifestyles.

The worsening economic situation, the continual occurrence of natural disasters and calamities and the effects of the political instability that characterized the past regimes have caused parallel shifts in societal structures, most especially in the family. The increasing incidence of women and men working overseas to eke out a living is one example of a social phenomenon that gave way to new types of family structures. More and more households are single-headed or women-headed as a result of the out-migration of Filipinos. House-sharing arrangements between and among single women, and live-in heterosexual or homosexual relation-ships, have also become viable options for urban living. This has, in many ways, contributed to the emerging shifts and variation in the traditional family. Nowadays, it is not uncommon to find women who may choose to live together or women who may prefer to be by themselves. Marriage, although it remains a strong institution, is no longer a convenient escape for the problems brought about by the pressures of traditional family life.

The influence of the media in the emerging changes in family structures cannot be understated. The media does perform its dual and com-plementary functions well: first, as creator of images and second, as reflector of images already operative and existing in contemporary society. The images have become more diverse and varied owing to the many cultural influences that beset contemporary urban life. Hollywood movies, trashy romantic novels and TV soap operas pandering to heterosexism are the main sources of entertainment, and these vulgarities are not often intercepted by alternative images and messages.

Despite these changes and shifts in societal structures and the increasing complexities brought about by urban existence, a lot of so-called traditionally held values remain intact. The emerging complex nature of modern life, especially in urban centres, may not necessarily mean that what has been traditionally construed as 'immoral' or 'sinful' has already transgressed such construction and achieved legitimate status. Heterosexism still works best when it is unspoken and unarticulated, because it takes on the form of a 'correct' moral posturing that could not even be challenged.

Lesbian lives

THE 'L' WORD: QUESTIONS ON IDENTITY AND IDENTIFICATION

I was not comfortable with the term 'lesbian' before. It's like a forbidden word, a taboo.[6]

I cannot call myself a tomboy, because it is a very specific term that doesn't fit me. For me, lesbianism is being woman-identified; at the same time, having strong feminist perspectives.[7]

Because of their incomprehensible absence in the history of Philippine civilization, lesbians find themselves in a loose and fluid position when it comes to self-identification. Unlike their gay male counterparts, Filipino lesbians do not have a wide array of terms that they can use to refer to themselves. Lesbians are in a real quandary in reconstituting their identities, as the term or word that could 'define' and capture their very existence is absent. Lesbian, dyke, tomboy, t-bird, *mars* and *pars*, magic, deviant, tibo, third sex, homo, closet king. These are some of the most common terms heaped upon women who choose to direct their energies to other women, emotionally, physically, politically and spiritually. Through the years, Filipino lesbians have increasingly adopted foreign terms and words to describe themselves, and are now becoming more comfortable with them.

Lesbians who have consistently disengaged themselves from the term 'lesbian' could not be expected to maintain serious conversation about the subject of lesbianism without being defensive or evasive about it. It is too often characteristically Filipino to avoid confrontation with issues that touch the sensitivity of many people. Lesbianism, because it is considered taboo and almost forbidden is not part of the ordinary discourse. In situations where it is discussed, it is usually in the form of gossip centred on identifying lesbians in the community and their existing relationships. These discussions do not adopt a serious tone. The technique employed to handle difficult issues such as sexuality is to trivialize it or make a joke out of it. Lesbians themselves are ill at ease discussing their own sexuality, reflecting a society that is unable to talk about sexuality and sex without being humorous or circumspect.

Similarly, there is a fierce resistance even among lesbians to call or label themselves as 'lesbian'. This could be attributed to the negative images that have been associated with the term. The word 'lesbian' may even prove too strong for women who have been in relationships with other women. Interestingly, women in butch/femme relationships vary in their self-identification: butches would consider themselves men, and femme-players do not, for most of the time, call themselves lesbian.

Labels have a distinct generational character. In the 1970s and up to the early 1980s, the terms t-bird, tomboy, tibo and third sex were the designated terms for the butch lesbian. In the late 1980s and early 1990s, more contemporary terms have evolved, such as *mars* (femme) and *pars* (butch), girl (femme) and magic (butch). It is very noticeable that the identification of the butch lesbian goes side by side with the femme lesbian. Through the years, the most enduring term used to refer to lesbians is tomboy. This is a catch-all phrase intended to describe lesbian identity, sexuality and behaviour. Tomboy is used to describe women who shake off ascribed feminine qualities such as modesty and passivity. Teenage girls who are into rough games and climbing trees; young women who sport masculine attire and mannerisms; women working in non-traditional jobs such as bus conductors, drivers, security guards and policewomen; and even a middle-aged unmarried woman who is seen in the constant company of another woman, all can be labelled as tomboys.

Femme lesbians are never referred to as tomboys, but the very absence of a specific term (other than girl or *mars*) to refer to their existence becomes manifest when out of sheer confusion people also label them as such. For women who subscribe to particular standards of identity, this labelling or name-calling can be potentially injurious, and could be misread as an insult to their femininity, an attribute that has remained intact throughout their relationship with another woman.

COMING OUT: NECESSITY OR BURDEN?

The issue of coming out has not surfaced as a necessity for lesbians until recently. Most do not recognize the need to come out, given the blanket of invisibility which envelopes their very existence. Invisibility performs a protective coating for lesbians. Spared the experience of dealing with and confronting their own existence, they can lead lesbian lives for twenty years without telling anybody, even themselves, that they are lesbians. Many lesbians think that provided they don't confront the issue of their sexual orientation and identity, they can partake of the privileges of the heterosexual world.

Filipinos are regarded as non-confrontative by nature. They strive to maintain good relations even at the cost of their own peace of mind. Lesbians who come out are seen as being confrontational about their self-identity, an attitude that is met with resistance by a culture that invests so much in establishing 'harmonious' relationships. Conformity is another operative value in interpersonal relationships. Coming out alters the existing harmony in relationships. Eventually, it also challenges and threatens what is being held as the operative mode. Some lesbians themselves react negatively to the issue of coming out. Such reaction springs from a notion that coming out is a Western concept that does not fit Philippine realities. In fact, this attitude is further corroborated by sociologists who say that lesbians would only bring about harm upon themselves if they were to come out.[8] Because they are invisible without exerting that much effort, why should they expose themselves to the dangers of being regarded as an outcast or deviant?

While lesbians are careful not to expose themselves to their families, they operate on two basic assumptions. Either their parents know that they are lesbians and they don't have to come out to them, or their parents do not know, and because of this there is no necessity to come out. Parents and families often represent the last stronghold for most lesbians. They may be out to the entire women's movement, to their close friends or peers, but not to their parents. Lesbians whose parents may have an inkling of their sexuality prefer to keep silent about it. Whether it is a result of living in a polite society, or because it is too undesirable a topic, or not part of the discourse, sexuality, specifically lesbianism, is never discussed at the dining table:

> Somehow I want to come out to my parents, but realistically I can't do it because I'm staying under their roof and there's a real possibility of getting kicked out (if they knew). There's no easy way to go about it. It's going to be shocking for them. We shouldn't confront it. Just try easing into a life of being together without having to say anything or calling attention to our being lesbians.[9]

This attitude is based on the premise that harmonious relations especially within the family, and particularly between children and parents, must always exist. It is considered a premium value in Philippine society. Thus, anything that is deemed 'unpleasant', challenging or threatening to the existing fabric of family relations is not viewed favourably. Lesbians feel that this trait is typically Filipino: to avoid discussing anything that might bring out one's worst fears or confirm one's worst suspicions. Parents are also more comfortable in 'rather not knowing'. Face to face with the truth about their children's sexuality, they would have to decide how their relations could proceed, and lesbians harbour real fears of being thrown out of the house, disinherited or disowned. On the other hand, some lesbians are indeed ready to come out but their parents or close relations choose to ignore the subject, despite their daughter's efforts to gain acceptance and support. It has almost become a national trait in this country to pride oneself on one's moral standing, with such morality based on Catholic precepts and doctrines and Church teachings and exhortations.

LESBIANS AND THE CATHOLIC CHURCH

The International Conference on Population and Development (ICPD) held in Cairo in September 1994 proved to be a landmark event for its unprecedented exposure of lesbian and gay issues. The Catholic Church used the occasion to proselytize its position on issues such as contraception, abortion and homosexuality, further manifesting its political force by calling for a mammoth rally, attended by thousands of school-children and adults. While the issue was more focused on attacks against the pro-choice positions of some members of the official delegation to the ICPD, the Church's foremost spokesperson, Jaime Cardinal Sin brandished admonitions that clearly spoke of hatred and intolerance towards pro-choicers, lesbians and other sexual minorities. In a letter addressed to parents, the Cardinal took the liberty of stating that '[the children] are being brainwashed to accept as normal, attractive and even glamorous certain abnormal and perverse sexual relationships and behaviour such as homosexuality, lesbianism, incest, oral sex, contraception, sterilization and abortion'.[10] This pastoral letter was read in all the Catholic churches in the country weeks before the Cairo conference was about to begin.

The letter drew mixed reactions and responses from both homosexuals and heterosexuals. A response from a group of lesbians who called themselves Concerned Lesbians in the Philippines was published in a national daily. It stated that the so-called pro-life principles of the Catholic Church are inconsistent in their encouragement of abuse, disrespect and intolerance for lesbians and gay men. Likewise, it was asserted that lesbians and gay men have as many rights as the next human being, and that they should be able to exercise these rights free from discrimination and persecution. The following is an excerpt from the statement:

> Homosexuality and lesbianism are valid options for loving and living, basic human rights based on free and intelligent choice, mutual respect and recognition of individual dignity. We enhance each other's capacity for compassion and humanity. We condemn and are campaigning against rape, incest and domestic violence. Only idiots and ignoramuses who cannot tell love and violence apart will mention their manifestations in one breath.[11]

The Catholic Church continues to exert its influence over the state, an arrangement which had been in place since the establishment of the Spanish colonial government. While there exists the principle of separation between church and state, the former does not hesitate to use force unashamedly whenever it feels it has the 'moral' obligation to do so. Filipinos are always reminded of the church's role in ending the twenty-year dictatorship of Ferdinand Marcos, and the prospect of another 'people power' revolution on the grounds of sexual morality or conservatism is not far-fetched.

Elements from the religious right have also started spreading their message, enforcing their campaigns of vilification more systematically. The number of born-again fundamentalist groups has steadily increased over the years, partly as an antidote to the increasing militancy of the populace against tyrannical regimes. These fundamentalist elements have infiltrated every village in the country, exploiting broadcast, print and alternative (street) media to propagandize their beliefs.

Me-ann, a lesbian from a rural barrio south of Manila, has been a member of various born-again groups ever since she felt that being a lesbian drove her away from God. Lesbianism, according to her belief, runs counter to the 'law of God' and the invitation of a born-again group offering refuge from her 'sinfulness' was an attractive option. However, she soon discovered that these born-again groups were of little help, and that in fact they made the situation worse by forcing her to change her ways and using guilt to 'reform' her. She mentioned that two of her lesbian friends who have been 'born again' are now preaching against lesbianism, delivering testimonies against it during services or gatherings. A troubling fact for most lesbians and gay men is that while they know they are involved in religious groups that do not recognize and accept them they are apparently unable to discern the hideous effects of this involvement. Religion uses guilt as its primary weapon, traumatizing women and men who do not fall within their 'moral' strictures:

> As a fourteen-year old teener, I remember having to feel guilty after having fantasies of making love with a women. I would always be comforted with the knowledge that I could go to confession any time and tell the priest that I was having 'impure' thoughts. [12]

It is no exaggeration to say that undue suffering and torment befalls the multitude of church believers and followers who have an ingrained sense of what is deemed necessary for their salvation or damnation. It is difficult to rationalize the reign of terror that the Church has inflicted on the individual and collective minds and consciences of its believers. It is, however, more appalling to know that most young women and men begin to have feelings of guilt at an early age, and carry this for the rest of their lives without understanding its basis. In a society that restricts the substance of allowable discourse, sexuality is a definite taboo, and any discussion on its merits and demerits rarely takes place sensibly and intelligently, free from the hysterics of its Catholic detractors.

While the Church no longer gets involved in bloody crusades to propagate its beliefs, it has succeeded in reigning over the minds and consciences of its subjects through verbal abuse, terror and threats of damnation. Cities outside the metropolitan Manila area are not spared from the Church's efforts to preach its mission against homosexuals. In Baguio City, located to the north of Manila, where a visible lesbian community exists, the Church has also resorted to the pulpit in its drive to rid the city of its 'immoral citizens'.[13]

It is not surprising, therefore, that the Metropolitan Community Church (MCC) has become the refuge and solace for a small but visible gay community. The MCC was established in 1992 and its membership is mainly composed of gay men. It came to prominence in 1994 when, in the heat of the ICPD, the Catholic Church came up with its condemnation of homosexual unions. The MCC also had its share of harassment and attacks. After its American minister's few appearances in a number of prominent TV shows, it received a notice of eviction from the owner of the house it was renting who had 'consulted' a monsignor about the morality of lesbian and gay marriages. Having been informed that these were wrong and fell outside the framework of the Catholic church, the owners barely gave the MCC time to pack and leave. By 1994, however, the MCC had officiated the first marriage of a lesbian couple.

LAWS AND LESBIANS

There is no specific law against lesbians or homosexuals. There are, however, laws with provisions that have a direct impact on lesbians and gays. One of these is the Family Code of the Philippines (EO No. 209), which was enacted into law in 1988. The Family Code partially repealed and superseded provisions on family relations contained in the Civil Code of the Philippines. The Family Code is the defining instrument of the family, and it protects relations between and among family members. Both codes contain the definition of marriage, but there has been a significant change in the wording of the definition. In Article 52 of the Civil Code, marriage is defined as

> not a mere contract but an inviolable social institution. Its nature, consequences and incidents are governed by law and not subject to stipulation, except that the marriage settlements may to a certain extent fix the property relations during the marriage.

This definition talks about marriage contracts in a general sense and only in reference to it as a legal and social institution. No reference is made as to who the contracting parties are. This definition of marriage is changed in Article 1 of the Family Code, which defines it as a special contract of *permanent union between a man and a woman* entered into in accordance with law for the establishment of conjugal and family life. It is the foundation of the family and an inviolable social institution whose nature, consequences, and incidents are governed by law and not subject to stipulation, except that marriage settlements may fix the property relations during the marriage within the limits provided by this code. (italics mine)

While it can be assumed that the old code refers to heterosexual unions, as certain provisions refer particularly to female/male relations, such an assumption is explicitly stated and evidenced in the new Family Code. Promulgated during the time of Corazon Aquino, a self-confessed god-fearing Catholic, the Family Code was proclaimed as a major legal achievement during her term of office. Aquino's regime relied heavily on the support of the Catholic Church, and it is not surprising that such laws would be enacted during her term of office.

The only specific reference to lesbianism and homosexuality in the Family Code occurs in the section on legal separation and annulment. Here, lesbianism and homosexuality are cited as grounds for legal separa-tion, along with physical violence, drug addiction, bigamous marriage, sexual infidelity or perversion. Likewise, concealed lesbianism or homo-sexuality are also considered grounds for annulment of marriage.

While heterosexual marriage has been debunked and repudiated by lesbians and some feminists, it remains an institution that is protected by all the social structures. Lesbians who are caught in a marriage may only be too happy to obtain legal separation or annulment, but in the eyes of the law they are the 'guilty' party. The case is filed against them, and if they have children, they may lose their rights to custody. On the other hand, because these provisions lump lesbianism alongside other grounds for annulment and legal separation, this clearly shows the extent to which lawmakers subject lesbian experience to prejudice and hate, without making any serious attempt to consider the validity of such experience. The premise of the provision is that marriage, at all costs, must be protected by church and state, and that it would need circumstances of a heinous character for it to merit a breakdown. Lesbianism is then given a *criminal* characteristic and becomes a reason to discontinue the marital relationship.

In the final analysis, however, heterosexism does not need a legal instrument for its institutionalization. Legislators and bureaucrats know that legislative discrimination is unconstitutional, and yet fear being directly associated with lesbian and gay rights. At the time of writing, there has been no proposed legislation sponsored in the Senate and Congress that concerns lesbian and gay rights. There are legislators who are rumoured to be gay, but given the climate of homophobia in Philippine society, coming out for a politician would be tantamount to political suicide. There are plans to put up a lesbian and gay force in the coming 1998 elections, and this project, if realized, could signal the start of a more visible movement for lesbian and gay rights.

THE EMERGENCE OF THE LESBIAN-FEMINIST MOVEMENT

Lesbians in the women's movement only began organizing in the early 1990s. While lesbianism had been a subject for discussion in a few women's organizations during the late 1980s, the women's movement was not ready to face the issue head-on, nor were lesbians prepared to organize autonomously as a specific group.Except for brief discussions on lesbianism in the context of women's sexuality and reproductive rights, no attempt was made to raise the issue to the level of discourse of other women's issues, such as health, reproductive rights and violence against women. An established woman academic who ventured into the meetings on reproductive health even posed the question, 'What do lesbians look like?'

Lesbian feminism is founded on the belief that lesbian relationships ultimately threaten and challenge the patriarchal and heterosexist pattern of the appropriation of women's bodies and lives for men. Heterosexuality ensures men's access to women's bodies; lesbians deny men such access.

Reactions among feminist activists and theoreticians were mixed when the young lesbians among them – between twenty and thirty years old – began initiating autonomous gatherings and activities. Differences in age, political experiences, social backgrounds, as well as the varied expressions of feminism within the women's movement, account for these diverse responses. While some quarters have supported lesbians organizing openly, other women have been known to make anti-lesbian remarks and statements in the presence of lesbians. Thus, during one organizational meeting of the NGOs, preparatory to an Asia-Pacific regional conference, one well-known woman leader was heard to ask, 'Should we include lesbians? That's the reason why our country is underdeveloped and impoverished. There is too much immorality.'

During preparatory activities for the Fourth United Nations World Conference on Women (held in Beijing in September 1995), lesbian issues were conspicuously absent from the agenda. Similarly, despite the efforts of a few lesbians to include lesbian issues from the beginning, no lesbian group was invited to get involved in the preparatory process. In the Asian and Pacific Symposium of NGOs on Women in Development (WID) – the first UN-sponsored regional NGO activity, preparatory to the Fourth World Conference on Women – only one participant (from Thailand) was able to come as an official representative of a lesbian group. The Asian Lesbian Network, a large coalition of Asian lesbians, was denied representation because 'it did not submit its application on time to meet the deadline'. During that conference, however, lesbian representatives from the different countries did meet and proposed a formal resolution from the floor during the plenary deliberations. Although it was said to have received the longest and loudest applause, the resolution was not incorporated in the final report.

The continued difficulty in getting lesbianism on the political agenda of the women's movement is but one of the many problems that beset the birth of the lesbian feminist movement. Some lesbian feminists conclude that, apart from feeling the strong need to come together as a visual articulation of lesbian existence, the initial organizing effort lacked a clear framework and understanding of lesbian issues in the context of feminism. Indeed, in the early stages of organizing work, lesbians tried to cater to varied perspectives on lesbianism because of the seeming diversity of the background of its participants.[14]

After the initial stages of laying down the groundwork for lesbian visibility, the women's movement has responded quite positively. The word 'lesbian' is being mentioned more often, and lesbian groups have finally gained access to the resources and connections of the more established women's networks and alliances. Women's groups are also starting to establish their own lesbian desks or support groups in their organizations, and to include lesbianism in their agenda and priority concerns.

It is interesting to note that given the fierce competition among women's organizations, the autonomous agenda of 'lesbian separatism' has never been raised. Sadly, a certain viciousness has characterized the relationship between a few lesbian groupings. As with any movement for social change, the lesbian feminist movement is not spared the problems that seem inherent in organizational politics. It is not difficult to see why some lesbian feminists would choose not to join lesbian organizations. They believe that the problems and conflicts permeating both the women's movement and the lesbian feminist movement are personality-

rather than issue-oriented.[15] But, while the petty battles rage on, the lesbian feminist movement is coming to terms with the need to establish links with international lesbian groups. This, in turn, has helped to give focus and direct attention to issues of the national lesbian struggle. Lesbian feminists have yet to decide which audience it will address, and how: the non-feminist lesbians, the women's movement or the male gay movement.

LESBIAN COMMUNITIES OUTSIDE THE MOVEMENT

Outside the confined boundaries of the lesbian feminist movement abound the so-called 'organic' lesbian communities or groups who make up the majority of the lesbian population. These lesbian groups are non-political in nature, and their organization has no direct connection to the women's movement or the human rights movement. These groups have existed and continue to exist even in the most far-flung areas, and have largely remained localized. The basis of unity for such organizations remains their sexuality and interpersonal relationships.

The most common purpose of such organizations is to function as a personal support system for other lesbians. These groups may have been deliberately organized by a lesbian who enjoys a high social standing in the community or well-established connections. It could also be a result of *pinagsamahan* – an experience of togetherness among some lesbians who see the formation of a group as a crystallizing force of their 'sister-hood'. The community has learned to accept them collectively, partly because they fulfil their functions and duties as 'lawful' citizens, and partly, too, because they do not make themselves a burden to the community as they engage in economically productive activities and are good providers to their families. Lesbian groups of this nature are not governed or guided by any lesbian feminist political framework. Most of their projects or endeavours may not have the political aim of advancing the struggle for lesbian rights or visibility, but the composition of their group is entirely lesbian.

Some of these groups also gain notoriety for being different and non-conformist in their lifestyle and behaviour. This is further compounded by the way in which some lesbians construe their self-identification to be male and live it according to patriarchal norms. In some ways, this could be seen as their way of coping and surviving in their own communities. There is one lesbian group in a province south of Manila which has earned a notorious reputation by engaging in rowdy drinking sessions and gambling sprees, to the consternation of their families. This group found an unlikely ally in the company of gay men.

Many non-feminist lesbians insist on perpetuating male/female dynamics in their relationships. The butch partner, or *pars*, acts out the male role, while the femme partner, or *mars*, acts out the female role. Thus, the dynamics of their relationship are derived from heterosexist patterns, with the *pars* functioning as the provider, in terms of economic and financial support. This role is even more pronounced in the sexual aspect of the relationship. The *pars* play out the male (dominant) role more pronouncedly in the sex act, priding themselves as the 'doers' or 'givers' in sexual intimacy.[16] This means that they alone are responsible for the sexual pleasure experienced by the *mars*, and therein lies the power, that they can be as equipped as 'real' men in making love to women. One of the most sacred tenets of this dynamic is that *pars* do not allow themselves even to be touched by their partner. To allow this would mean becoming 'women' themselves, and as 'women' they would be stripped of their power over the *mars* in the relationship. The *pars* provokes awe while posturing as a man, with male privilege and power extended to her as part of the illusion.

Pars have their own ethics, with an unspoken policy to check on each other, making sure that they do not succumb to 'feminine' tendencies. The basic assumption of this dynamic centres on how the *pars* defines her sexual identity. Clearly, she acknowledges her maleness in all spheres of her existence and begrudges the 'female' in her which is solely predetermined by her biological anatomy. Also, because of this male identification, spaces traditionally defined as male-dominated also become the territories of lesbians. Work that involves manual labour, or that entails risks and physical danger, attracts *pars*, who believe that they can perform as well as men.

The differences in definition and construction of sexual identity between lesbian feminists and non-feminist identified lesbians have unwittingly demarcated a line between the two. Most non-politicized lesbians strictly enforce sex/gender roles, partly because they cannot conceive of a world outside of a heterosexist model. Likewise, they view their lesbianism as too threatening a fact, and find it more helpful to operate in a framework that is still familiar and comprehensible. Role-playing then assumes the function of the harmonizer, as the community that they deal with will be able to comprehend their 'non-conformist' lifestyle. As one lesbian put it, 'As lesbians, we are already confused, how much more if we operate without established roles?'[17]

One other area of difference between non-feminist lesbians and lesbian feminists is the way lesbian origins are perceived. Non-feminist lesbians speak of being born gay, that is, their lesbianism is inborn or organic, and that at no point in their lives did they feel any attraction to men. This realization that no conscious choices were made to become gay has a dual effect. First, it serves as a positive confirmation for those who have been able successfully to come to terms with their sexuality. Second, for those who had to grapple continuously with the reality of being lesbians, the agony becomes inscrutable. Lesbians experience a sense of being trapped and disjointed, unaware or uninformed of the affirming nature of lesbian feminist consciousness. It is said that non-feminist lesbians who have since joined the movement speak of a renewed affirmation of their lesbian existence, bolstered by a framework that has helped them come to terms with their sexual identity.

Lesbian feminists, on the other hand, speak of their lesbianism as a conscious political choice, in that their option to direct their lives to women is born out of concrete feminist analyses and a turning away from heteropatriarchy. In some cases, though, the conscious political choice has become an overly self-conscious label, to the extent that some have arrogated the term 'lesbian' to refer exclusively to lesbian feminists. While lesbian feminists frown on the *pars/mars* or butch/femme imagery as a product of heteropatriarchy, many have come to acknowledge that this self-righteous attitude is condescending and discriminatory to non-feminist lesbians. Instead of encouraging collaboration, this self-righteousness succeeds rather in alienating the greater number of women who could form the body of the lesbian rights movement.[18]

NEGATIVE STEREOTYPES

One reason why lesbian feminists have opted to separate from the dominant *pars/mars* mould is the negative representation of lesbians in the media and the bad publicity given by the straight community to 'main-stream' lesbians. A quick survey of locally produced films and TV pro-grammes reveals the limited and faulty representation of lesbians. In these productions they are commonly portrayed as rough thugs who just need a man to sweep them off their feet. They could experience endless adventures as lesbians, but they always end up marrying the 'hero' of the story.

The very few portrayals of lesbians in print and broadcast media is resounding proof of society's resistance to confront lesbian existence. Gay men, on the other hand, enjoy unparalleled publicity status in the print and broadcast media, appearing as entertainment columnists, showbiz personalities or beauty/fashion consultants, areas that have traditionally been defined as female territory. In the media, gay men are given prime-time exposure, a tacit acknowledgement or acceptance of their identities. Unfortunately, this acceptance is not unconditional, as their visibility is also grounded in ridicule. Almost all primetime local TV sitcoms have gay male characters, who fulfil the role of town mascot, community laughing-stock or the antidote to the macho man. The parody is not without malice, and even emphasizes the invisibility of true-to-life female roles, as well as the negative visibility of women.

Another theme that is most commonly attributed to lesbians focuses on their violent behaviour. Lesbians, like the men they ape, are potential criminals. But unlike the men, they cannot be respectable, they cannot be given positive roles and images. There is a very strong case, then, for lesbian feminists to resist the perpetuation of these images by dissociat-ing with 'mainstream' lesbians, either in public or in private or by strongly emphasizing the absence of sex roles in their relationships. At the same time, however, it is recognized that in the final analysis, and that despite the *pars/mars* dynamic, this involves two women relating to each other and as such should be considered in political organizing work.

STRUGGLE FOR AUTONOMY: LESBIANS AND GAY MEN

One other arena that lesbian feminists are starting to examine is the relationship with the gay male movement. Interaction and dialogues have started quite recently between lesbian and gay groups, but there has not been any serious attempt to come together and form more cohesive unions or alliances. Lesbian feminists are acutely aware that they have their own issues autonomously from gay men. Although the door towards co-operation and co-ordination with gay men has not been closed, the issue of forging actual alliances or linkages with gay men remains un-addressed. An atmosphere of support for each other's causes is main-tained, and at the same time an openness to the possibilities of working together is sustained by some lesbian groups.

One of the basic differences between the struggle waged by the lesbians *vis-à-vis* the gay groups is that gay men do not need to fight for visibility. Gay men enjoy a certain status of acceptance and visibility, albeit limited to *parloristas* and couturiers, that does not extend to lesbians. This gives them a head start in the gay rights struggle. Although it may be argued that such acceptance may be grounded on ridicule or stereotyping, the fact remains that gay men do exist in the eyes of a society that gives sole premium to male experience.

That the gay men's movement is more diverse than the lesbian feminist movement is attested to by the presence of groups with varying perspectives and political persuasions. Openly gay men have more access to funding, resources and positions of influence; they have also come to the forefront of the safe-sex and HIV/AIDS campaign, two issues that have become a priority of the Philippine government and the Department of Health (DOH). The DOH had been working hand in hand with gay groups on issue awareness on HIV/AIDS and safe-sex education.

The same cannot be said of lesbians, who still have to find a government body that would champion lesbian rights in the same manner and with as much vigour as it has with the HIV/AIDS campaign. Although not a campaign for gay rights, the act of collaboration with the gay men's movement concretely manifests the credibility and acceptability that gay men have established with an important government institution. Some gay groups, however, would still dispute this, believing that while high-profile gay men have gained social acceptance in powerful circles – including the inner circle of the President's First Lady – the struggle for gay rights still has a long way to go.

Another point of departure between lesbians and gay men concerns reproductive health issues, which the latter seem oblivious to. Since most lesbian activists operate within the framework of feminism, the indifference of gay men to such issues becomes a clear dividing point. During the drafting of the gay and lesbian statement on the Cairo conference, gay men's groups initially even agreed with the Church's position that contraception and abortion were 'evils' to be lumped together with rape and incest, while protesting that homosexuality should have been made an exception.

Lesbians have learned that one cannot take for granted a feminist perspective when it comes to dealing with gay men. Although there is a common cause and enemy, ultimately power politics between males and females comes into the picture, and gay men have often resorted to their age-old male privilege. Most gay men have in fact carried anti-women and misogynous attitudes. This is a reality that the lesbian and gay groups have to face. Lesbians will still have to bear the torch of their own struggle, as lesbians and as women.

HOW PROGRESSIVE IS THE PROGRESSIVE MOVEMENT?

The Philippine left, also known as the Progressive movement – or more specifically the national democratic, or 'ND' movement, as differentiated from leftist individuals or organizations working generally outside the established socio-political order – continues to wage its propaganda war against the state, amidst its own recent internal polarization of leadership and ideological struggles. A legacy of Ferdinand Marcos's rule, and even Cory Aquino's regime, it continues to manifest itself as the dominant human rights community and to assert its presence in Philippine politics, an arduous task given the new issues and interests taken up by activists, such as violence against women, ecology, drug abuse and HIV/AIDS.

The emergence of these issues, and of late the lesbian and gay struggle, has brought into question the existing framework and analysis of the left. The challenge to reconstruct the framework of human rights to include women's rights and lesbian and gay rights has been raised on many occasions. However, because the Philippine left and the human rights community stubbornly cling to the definition of human rights violations as those perpetrated by the state and military against its political adversaries, no human rights organization has exerted any effort to expand its concerns. Dialogues and discussions have not achieved much.

The ND movement has had a long history of homophobia. A former woman leader of its guerrilla army relates how one's sexuality can become a reason for failure to rise up the ranks of the leadership in the underground. As late as the mid-1980s lesbians and gay men continued to be the subject of a non-stop harangue, enduring relentless admonitions to change to a heterosexual lifestyle. The absence of an official policy paper on lesbianism and homosexuality further clouded the basis for some actions within the movement to address the issue of lesbianism and homosexuality.

Homophobia was concretely manifested during the process of self-criticism, a Maoist approach to self-evaluation, applied by the left and most especially the underground movement. The original intent of this process was to be able to assess one's work and performance within the movement, but it also took the form of a self-assessment of one's weaknesses and strengths. Lesbianism and homosexuality fell under the 'weakness' category that had to be overcome by the self-confessed *cadre*. Thus, a reorientation to heterosexuality, or deliberate desisting from homosexual or lesbian practice, was often arrived at as a resolution by the self-confessed lesbians and gay men so that they could function as bona fide *cadres* of the revolutionary underground or left.

Through the efforts of the women, there have been reported changes in the attitudes and outlook of the left concerning issues of sexuality, and a recent lesbian formation has been organized. How far this change in attitude will go remains to be seen.

THE BALAY CASE: HUMAN RIGHTS AGAINST LESBIAN RIGHTS

A well-known case of discrimination against two lesbians in the human rights community confirms the inability of the so-called progressive movement to reconstruct their framework to include lesbian and gay rights. On 6 September 1994, Evangeline Castronuevo and Elizabeth Lim, both workers at the Balay Rehabilitation Centre, were dismissed from their jobs after coming out about their relationship. Balay is a human rights organization offering direct services for political prisoners and other state victims of human rights violations. Prior to their dismissal, the two women had received a positive evaluation of their work in Balay. Their termination took effect on the same day that they received the notice.

While there is a clear absence of due process in the manner in which the decision to dismiss the women was reached, the grounds for termination remain questionable and bereft of legal basis. Such grounds were couched in Balay's 'concern' at the supposed breakup of Castronuevo's marriage, following the revelation of her relationship with Lim. The institution claimed that the issue was Castronuevo's extramarital relationship, and the two women's flaunting of it. Balay, however, showed no concern over another woman worker's extramarital relationship with a man. Likewise, the matter of flaunting remains contentious: by what standards does one define flaunting? Or as defined by Balay, does that include the act of accompanying one's lover to buy lunch? The two women were also chastised for 'lobbying for support from women's organizations', a charge that sounds ludicrous, coming from a human rights organization. Castronueuo and Lim have since filed charges against the Balay Rehabilitation Centre with the Department of Labour. The case is ongoing and it has been reported on and documented as the first case of discrimination against lesbians filed in the Philippine courts. The affair has also spawned the formation of a support network of lesbian groups and women's groups called Advocates for Lesbian Rights (Alert), which is working for the resolution of the case.

The silence of the human rights community on the case confirms that the rights of women and sexual minorities have not been included in the agenda of human rights groups, and further proves the homophobia of the Philippine left. Alert has not received any formal response or statement of support from a single human rights organization. Ironic as it may seem, the 'progressive' ideologues of our society will, however, readily don armour and battle gear to defend the traditional superiority of the hetero-sexual and patriarchal order. In this particular case, Castronuevo's former marriage was given priority over her relationship with Lim, even if the facts make it clear that her marriage could no longer be salvaged. Apparently, a heterosexual marriage, no matter how violent and destructive, should always be stitched and mended. But a lesbian union, and a happy and fulfilling one at that, deserves to be ripped apart.

As the first suit filed in court against an employer for discrimination on the basis of sexual orientation, Castronuevo and Lim's case will set the precedent for the lesbian rights struggle in the legal sphere. Theirs is a saga for the brave and the courageous. Other stories of this kind remain untold.

Postscript: lesbian thread

The Philippines is an archipelago composed of 7,000 islands, more than 300 ethno-linguistic groups and eight major languages. It has a rich and diverse culture, not unified by a single thread but by thousands of intermingling strands criss-crossing and locking into each other. It is also a culture that has borne silent witness to lesbian existence and will continue to do so until the knots of the dominant heterosexual culture are broken loose by lesbian weavers spinning ancient and contemporary tales as part of the vibrant tapestry of our people. Slowly, the strands are coming together. The process will bring pain, just as it will take daring. But the task has begun.

ACKNOWLEDGEMENTS

Seventeen lesbians of varying ages, political persuasions, class and ethnic origins were interviewed for this article. Most of them who contributed vital first-hand information or shared experiences for this article will have to remain anonymous for the moment, until the time comes when the public is ready to accept them and their statements without recrimination.

They know who they are, and I thank them profusely. Many thanks also to Anna Leah Sarabia for her editing skills.

NOTES

1. Interview with Dr Carol Sobritchea, Professor of Philippine Studies, University of the Philippines, Diliman, Quezon City, Philippines.
2. Conversations with members of UGAT (Ugnayan Agham Tao), Anthropological Society of the Philippines, August 1994.
3. Interview with Dr Ma. Luisa Camagay, Associate Professor of Philippine History, University of the Philippines, Diliman, Quezon City, Philippines.
4. Interview with Laura Samson, Professor of Sociology, University of the Philippines, Diliman, Quezon City, Philippines.
5. *Ibid.*
6. Interview with 'Cathy'.
7. Interview with D.
8. Interview with Laura Samson.
9. Interview with 'Dawn'.
10. Pastoral letter of Jaime Cardinal Sin, read at all churches weeks before the Cairo conference.
11. Statement by CLIC, for 'Concerned Lesbians in the Philippines' published in *Today*, 16 August 1994.
12. Interview with 'Randy'.
13. Interview with Julie Palaganas, member of Lesbond, a lesbian group in Baguio City.
14. Interview with Tesa de Vela, founding member of The Lesbian Collective, a lesbian feminist group formed in 1993.
15. Interview with S. S., a closet lesbian feminist.
16. Interview with Portia Ilagan, one of the first lesbians who came out in the Philippines during the 1980s.
17. Interview with R., a non-aligned, non-political lesbian.
18. Interview with Tesa de Vela.

GLOSSARY

Babaylan: priestess or spiritual healer.
Balay: home or place.
Cadre: bona fide member of the guerrilla movement.
Datu: ruling chieftain.
Mars: femme lesbian, originally from the Spanish word *madre*.

Parlorista: term for gay male beauticians or hairdressers who work in beauty parlours.

Pars: butch lesbian, originally from the Spanish word *padre*.

Pinagsamahan: experience of togetherness.

3 jami or lesbian?

giti thadani

Anti-lesbian mythology

This chapter is a general examination and deconstruction of the different heterosexual myths that prevail in India. These myths have acted as major blocks to the creation of autonomous lesbian cultures. I also provide a brief chronicle of the nascent lesbian feminist activism, its history and the contemporary context in which it occurs.

THE MYTH OF LESBIAN NON-EXISTENCE

> There is no such thing in India. It has come from the West through these new [Indian] films. (Comment from a TV programme on homosexuality in India, July 1994)

This statement was made after lesbian images from various 'Indian' historical traditions had been shown. It was then followed by another statement saying that in effect 'it' had been declared illegal and thus eradicated by Manu (approx. 1000–500 BC).

One of the most conventional myths in India is that any form of lesbianism is a product of Western decadence. However, if one analyses this, a number of contradictions emerge. First, there is the inability to use the word 'lesbian' or any other equivalent term, an incapacity to accord a name that functions as a blanket denial of lesbianism within Indian traditions. However, the second statement contradicts this by alluding to 'its' existence in the remote past when it was declared illegal by 'Manu', the first man.

Clearly, such statements are not concerned with any kind of objective reality or evidence. The new Indian films are as heterosexual as before, and Indian histories remain replete with evidence of lesbian sexualities. In effect, it remains to be asked what lies behind the obsessive reiteration that lesbian sexuality is the property of the 'Western' other. Is this really a myth or rather, in its persistent repetition, is it merely one of the techniques of deliberate heterosexual propaganda which refuses any kind of engagement with 'Indian' lesbian histories.

If one analyses the above statements further, another underlying sub-text emerges, namely that lesbianism existed but was subsequently eradicated after being declared a criminal activity. It is only now, with the opening of geographical boundaries, that 'it' can re-enter the 'pure hetero-sexual Indian' world. One of the major ideologies of purity is found in the caste system. This is consistent with concepts of purity associated with brahmanism, where it was only the foreign 'other' which could pollute the carefully contained 'pure' caste system. Lesbianism, no doubt, is conceived as a major pollutant. This is also evident in the laws of Manu:

> A kanya who does it to another kanya must be fined 200 panas, pay the double of the bride price and receive ten lashes of the rod. But a stri who does it to a kanya shall instantly have her head shaved or two fingers cut off and be made to ride through the town on a donkey. (Laws of Manu 8.369 and 370)

Categories of age are clearly demarcated in the above laws. *Kanya* connotes a young girl virgin, whereas *stri* refers to a mature woman. Whereas the first 'offence' requires physical punishment and financial compensation of the father, that of the older woman is seen as much more dangerous. The act of shaving the head or severing two fingers is a form of sexual castration, and the enforced ride through the town on a donkey represents an act of public humiliation, ostracism and exile.

But what do the above laws mean in today's context? Do they belong to a remote past or are they so deeply internalized that there is no need for an external law system? Yet an external law does exist. This was implemented in the nineteenth century in India by the British. The main text of the law is that any 'sexuality against the order of nature' is punishable, the maximum punishment being life imprisonment. Further, as it constitutes a criminal offence, it does not qualify for bail. However, when the law was instituted in Victorian England and subsequently in India, lesbian sexuality was inconceivable. Legislation was aimed rather at the act of sodomy and bestiality with animals.

For a long while no attention was paid to the current implications of the law, as reportedly very few sentences had been given and then only in cases of sodomy. It seemed to pose no danger to lesbians and is still thought of today as an anti-sodomy law. On closer examination it was found that only those cases which had come to the level of the higher court were recorded. Further, as the 'offence' does not qualify for bail the 'offender' may be arrested and languish in prison until such time as the case is decided – which could be many years. This means that the law can be used as a mechanism of coercion against individuals, with lesbians being no exception. The following case was reported in the magazine India Today on 15 April 1990:

> Tarulata changed her sex to marry her girl friend, Lila Chavda. Muljibhai Chavda, Lila's father, went to the Gujurat High Court, saying that as it was a lesbian relationship, the marriage be annulled. Criminal action was called for under the above law. The writ petition contended that 'Tarunkumar (Tarulata) possesses neither the male organ nor any natural mechanism of cohabitation, sexual intercourse and procreation of children. Adoption of any unnatural mechanism does not create malehood and as such Tarunkumar is not a male.'

The petition was accepted by the court. No further information is known.

The issues that the above law raises are manifold, as the term 'sexuality against the order of nature' lends itself open to many very dubious interpretations. Previously it was only the act of 'phallic penetration' which constituted the *raison d'être* of the law. Now, when grounded in an earlier brahmanic and caste ideology, the law becomes an establishment of 'correct gender codes', the result of earlier internalized laws on 'right sexuality and gender codes': 'When there is the non-penetrative act, then there is no progeny and thus it is jami; two men or women sleeping together' (sacrificial texts). It is only procreative sex that is desirable and constitutive of 'right sexuality'. Furthermore, only this form of sexuality established the desired gender identities of virile malehood and docile womanhood. Any kind of gender fluidity was seen as dangerous, as a form of possession by the dark goddess Nirrti: 'That woman having a male form and that male having a woman's form are possessed by Nirrti.' (Sacrificial texts.)

The internalization of this ideology is very clear in the Tarulata case. The gender cross-over is not enough to establish malehood, but nonreproductive sexuality is sufficient to constitute 'abnormality'. Tarulata can therefore never be a 'normal' man, and for that reason is incapable of 'normal = procreative sex'. Whatever the legal decision, the fact that the high court accepted the case is enough to establish the coercive nature of the law.

Activists have reported cases of the threatened enforcement of the law to break up lesbian relationships. This is very difficult to document, however, as the inner stigmatization and fear of public humiliation, which is tantamount to ostracism and exile, will remain until a conscious lesbian identity and subculture develops. The fear of the public implications of the law, the stigma of being labelled a 'criminal', constitutes a double form of victimization. Any form of anti-lesbian violence is never reported, although there have been known cases of lesbian battering, rape within the family by male members, as well as murder. The major psycho-social implication of the law is that the lesbian, iconized as a criminal and abnormal, has no recourse to any kind of retribution and justice for the violence meted out to her. Needless to say, the supposed sacredness of the heterosexual family results in the silencing and condoning of rape and violence within its sanctity, and yet it remains the symbol of eternal Indianness, whereas any form of homosexuality is attributed to the immoral and decadent West. The following letter, which appeared in the daily newspaper *The Pioneer* on 12 November 1992, aptly sums up this attitude:

CALL THE COPS

Sir

It is surprising that your paper should publish a photograph of protesting gays. This is a contemptible and immoral conduct. We don't have to ape all what goes on in the West. Today homosexuality is legal and acceptable there, and soon it will be accepted as normal conduct here as well.

'Gays' is a fashionable word for an unnatural offence and is punishable as a crime. Our police could have rounded up those appearing in the photograph as propagating unnatural acts. I hope the police gets moving now.

J. Mohan, New Delhi.

THE MYTH OF (HETEROSEXUAL) ECONOMIC DEVELOPMENT

The second anti-lesbian myth holds that as a developing nation India has other more pressing problems, such as overpopulation, poverty, illiteracy, communalism, etc., and therefore that economic issues have to be seen as far more important than issues around women's sexual choices and kinship. Whereas the first myth posits the lesbian as a Western creation, the second, which is the basic stance of the dominant left and feminist movements, sees the need for lesbian rights as the expression of only a few Westernized, individualistic and economically independent women. In other words, lesbian feminist activity is seen as a privilege that only a handful can afford.

No attempt is made, however, to understand how such issues as overpopulation, poverty, illiteracy and communalism are all linked to the ideologies and structures of compulsory heterosexuality, wherein women's sexuality and the right to any sexual choice and pleasure is strictly taboo. Women are regarded as mere producers of boy children, who are seen as constitutive of rural and urban capital. And the heterosexual family, which is the basic institution of the above, is never brought into question. As one of the major components of heteropatriarchy, it is crucial in maintaining the division of labour and thus the structuring of external and internal economies. Whereas the external economy is located in social and public spaces, the internal functions at the private and domestic level. This means that women do far more work in terms of the maintenance of the family and society, but do not control the resources.

The heterosexual family also functions as the only visible expression of sexuality. Here, only procreative sexuality is seen as necessary. And within this framework only male sexuality is seen as significant. It is constructed as penetrative and as discharge, with women adopting the role of passive receivers. This aspect of male sexuality, i.e. penetration and discharge, is what is sublimated in the mass male movements of the right, the left and anything in between. Public space is again dominantly male.

This construction also presupposes that to receive any kind of support women must be victims and cannot aspire to be autonomous, erotically affirmed and visible sexually, particularly if they are lesbians. The victim space is occupied with arrogance by heterosexual women (and men), but any acknowledgement of women's self-determination or affirmation, particularly of sexual identity is seen as dangerous, selfish, individualistic and elitist. Thus, the only terminology and identity used to describe women outside marriage is that of an asexual single woman.

THE MYTHS OF LIBERAL TOLERANCE: THE MODERN INDIAN SECULAR CITY

The development of the modern metropolitan city has enabled the development of a middle class as well as that of a liberal secular culture. Though there is no comparison to the freedom that the modern city provides, liberal discourse creates other myths and stereotypes of tolerance which are equally repressive, though much more subtle. The first liberal myth claims that as homosociality is accepted, it is less of a problem for two lesbian women living together than for unmarried heterosexual couples. This ignores the fact that acceptance is only forthcoming because the homosocial relationship is presumed to be non-sexual. The moment the sexual aspects of the relationship become visible, the acceptance ceases and the lesbian couple more often than not is excommunicated. In the case of the unmarried heterosexual couple, there is always the choice of social visibility and legitimacy.

Whereas homosocial and homoemotive spaces are more of an accepted reality than the heterosocial or heteroemotive, they are subsumed by the economy of the heterosexual family, and are seen as a sometimes necessary passage to heterosexual marriage. The heterosexual marriage is a complex social institution based on a pact which is an exchange of spaces. In the brahmanical marriage ceremony seven vows are chanted. The first six constitute what the man must provide for his wife, namely financial and other forms of security. The seventh and last vow is that the woman forfeits all rights to her independence. The moment homosociality between women becomes homosexual as well, it transgresses the economy of heterosexuality and the elaborate apparatus of the extended Indian family. It can only be reincorporated when the sexual aspects are veiled. Acceptance may follow, but only if one can be subsumed within the family economy, at best as a devoted daughter, sister or eccentric aunt.

The issue of tolerance may then be posed in other terms, as a form of exchange which maintains the conspiracy of silence and of non-articulation of an autonomous lesbian identity. What this presumes is the invisibility of women as sexual beings, independent from male desire. It leads to women having a closet existence, which is often the desired option for it allows access to heterosexual privilege. There are a number of ways that women live out this existence: many are married and have a women lover on the side; or, if economically privileged, they live the heterosexual experience in India while experimenting with lesbian relationships in the West. They swing between heterosexual and lesbian behaviour, where heterosexuality represents social security and status and is the facade behind which sexual behaviour with women may be lived out sporadically, providing, of course, that it does not threaten the heterosexual existence. This is accompanied by the belief that there can be lesbian behaviour but no lesbian identity; the dominant identity must be either the wife, mother or the single asexual woman. In addition, there can be no women-centred kinship: women lovers cannot and should not live out their relationship in a visible and honest manner. Silence about lesbian behaviour and dishonesty to partners (female and male) is seen as necessary and often erotically enhancing.

These attitudes and behaviours are linked to the second myth of liberal tolerance. This holds that categories of gender are more fluid in Indian cultures, therefore one does not need overt declarations of sexual identities which function as restricting rather than liberating. Mixed gender spaces are the answer and the norm. Bisexuality is seen as the freest sexual choice. Needless to say, in this world it is only the heterosexual option that may be openly lived out.

This myth advocates the creation of a heteroemotive space in addition to the heterosexual space. However, it does not advocate the inverse: that a free space exist for the lesbian homoerotic and homosexual in addition to the homosocial and homoemotive. Instead, it is advocating the forfeiting and dismantling of a feminine homosocial space in order for a heterosocial space to be developed. In other words, this means that men be allowed to access women-only social spaces but retain male dominance in the public sphere as well as male-only spaces.

However, ancient tales testify to the women-only spaces that have traditionally existed in Indian society. One of these tales relates how, during the absence of the male god Shiv (who is on one of his possibly philanderous rampages), the goddess Parvati creates out of her own fluid, as a form of parthenogenesis, the androgynous god Ganesh. The main function of Ganesh is to act as the doorkeeper, preventing the entry of any man into Parvati's women-only space. When Shiv returns he too is denied access and in a fit of rage beheads Ganesh. Parvati is furious and threatens to take on her wrathful Kali form and revenge herself, when eventually a reconciliation is reached. Ganesh is given a new head – an elephant head, which represents matriarchy and matrilineality.

The narrative displays a very complex use of gender codes. Parvati, though supposedly in a heterosexual arrangement, does not forfeit her autonomous feminine space. Rather she creates an androgynous male doorkeeper. However, even this androgynous male figure cannot enter into her feminine space, but rather has the role of keeping other men out. The women-only space is seen as a fluid space (where Parvati bathes with other women), free from male gaze and desire.

These women-only spaces still exist in many places. The supposedly liberal voice that advocates the dismantling of these spaces also subtly negates the need and right for women to have privacy from the male gaze. Thus, far from being located only at an individual level, the issue of lesbian rights and identities has a much wider socio-political significance. For a fluid women's space to emerge there would have to be a consciousness of one's sexuality and a space free from the male gaze in order to develop and free lesbian sexuality and its positive expression.

What the myth of tolerance perpetuates in a very subtle way is the maintenance of a loss of identity and a forfeiting of any open, holistic, emotional and sexual bonding between women. It also negates the need for autonomous spaces of exchange between women which are not an appendage to the extended heterosexual family. At a collective level, it individualizes the lesbian relationship as a private, isolated phenomenon, devoid of any social and historical context. Tolerance becomes equal to assimilation. The price of non-assimilation is to become non-Indian. In other words, lesbians are exiled the moment they aspire to any sexual and kinship visibility. This is in accordance with the earlier law of being excommunicated in the caste system, which was synonymous with slow death in the face of total isolation. In this context it is easy to understand how the statement that there are 'no lesbians in India' is part of a deliberate technique of excommunication, whereby the identity of Indian-ness becomes representative of a totalitarian heterosexual order.

Lesbian visibility and feminist activism

In recent years metropolitan cities have witnessed the rise of women professionals. Although confined to the development of the middle class, this has resulted in a somewhat freer climate and the gradual emergence of independent women's lifestyles. The hitherto veil of silence that surrounded homosexuality is slowly being lifted by the media, both negatively and positively. One of the first affirmative visible actions was the publication of the magazine *Bombay Dost* in 1990. The first issue stated that its aim was to provide a platform for articulating positive forms of alternative sexuality. Alternative sexualities were defined as those other than that of normative heterosexuality. Initially, the collective included both men and women. However, the name of the magazine clearly indicated a male bias: *dost* means male friend. The masculine nature of the name testifies to the magazine's gay male domination, though it still remains one of the few forums for lesbian articulation within India.

SAKHI

In 1990, a statement was issued by a group of Delhi-based lesbians under the title of Sakhi. Whereas earlier, in certain kinds of Sanskrit, the word *sakhi* was expressive of an erotic and sexual relationship between women, it has currently become desexualized and signifies non-sexual friendship between women. The usage of the word in association with 'lesbian' was a way of overturning an ideology that is set on the desexualization of women friendships, that identifies lesbian practices and lifestyles as a Western phenomenon, that believes the word 'lesbian' to have no meaning in an Indian context, and that equates the lack of Indian vocabulary relating to lesbians with the non-existence of lesbianism itself. The salient points contained in the group's statement included the necessity of networking, the creation of lesbian visibility, the challenging of anti-lesbianism, the internalization of heterosexual roles even within lesbian relationships and the demarcation of its differences with the gay male movement. It also challenged the contemporary feminist, left and civil rights movements over their silence on lesbian issues.

The contemporary feminist movement, which started in the early 1980s, has thematized various issues such as rape, the dowry etc., but has internalized both the sexophobia and lesbophobia of society as a whole. Although the movement has provided a space for women to interact with each other, it still maintains for the most part that any open lesbian declaration will endanger the cause. This has led to the perpetuation of a closeted lesbian culture, which maintains that any open lesbian identity is the prerogative of the 'first world' but remains unsuitable for a 'developing country' where other issues are more important. This has meant that there have been major public campaigns around reproductive sexuality, but not on lesbianism or the right to sexual choice.

One of the major difficulties that has emerged in the relationship with the gay male movement is the prevalence of misogyny and sexism. Furthermore, gay men have more resources as well as easier access to public space than women. In Bombay, after a certain time of the day an entire train operates as a gay local. Needless to say, there are hardly any women in local trains at night. The lack of access to safe and public spaces is fundamentally a lesbian issue as it increases isolation, a fact that was born out by the response to Sakhi's statement in the form of a slow trickle of letters from women all over the country. The common thread in all these letters was a terrible sense of isolation and the overwhelming need to make some kind of contact. Many of the women who wrote in were married. Many came from small towns where there was next to no possibility of any existence outside marriage. Some of the letters received spoke of coercive family pressure to marry. Many related the dilemma of having to sacrifice their own lesbian desire for family duty and the maintenance of family honour. Some writers saw suicide as the only option to forced marriage.

Curiously, one of the other major factors responsible for breaking the media silence on homosexuality was the advent of HIV/AIDS. Initially the Indian state had tried to deny its presence by maintaining its claims to heterosexual purity. A top medical official went so far as to call for legislation against sex with foreigners. (Later, due to the money being pumped in by international agencies, the HIV/AIDS 'industry' became a lucrative business for some corrupt bureaucrats.) In 1992 a major international HIV/AIDS conference was held in New Delhi. The intention seemed to be much more to promote tourism then any meaningful discussion of either the implications of HIV/AIDS or an open discussion of sexuality. The description of homosexuality as deviant and perverse in some of the brochures led to the organization of the first open meetings around lesbian and gay issues.

Although the conference was attended by many more men than women, it was in recent urban history the first open gay and lesbian event and brought about a much-needed visibility. It also provided for a different kind of common platform where lesbian and gay activists could discuss issues such as sexual choice and discrimination, resistance to heterosexual marriage, family emotional blackmail and affirmative non-heterosexual lifestyles and identities. One of the major obstacles to any lesbian and gay movement has been the family culture: the emotional pressure to marry for both sexes is overwhelming. As stated earlier, families often agree only to accept homosexual behaviour provided the facade of heterosexuality is maintained. Needless to say, this is very detrimental to the building of any positive identity and lifestyle.

The meetings attracted a great deal of media attention. Although sometimes anti-lesbian, the visibility generated was on the whole positive, particularly given the earlier context of embarrassed silence. It was as if the open and self-affirmed lesbian and gay presence highlighted the need to break many taboos relating to the overall sexophobic climate. A small public demonstration also took place within the conference, questioning lesbophobia and homophobia. And a small group of activists working around issues of discrimination in relation to HIV/AIDS extended their actions to the issues of sexual discrimination and choice.

Just prior to the conference, Sakhi had set up a small archive and drop-in centre. The visibility generated by the events surrounding the conference led to the dissemination of the group's address in the national press, which resulted in a greater inflow of letters. A small library was established, which housed various kinds of documentation, including local newspaper cuttings, older historical material and international literature. One of the main objectives of the resource centre was to initiate research into different lesbian historical traditions, thus creating a socio-historical context. This was seen as vital to developing affirmative identities which were relevant to the Indian context and non-Eurocentric. This would then permit a better understanding of the different kinds of international literature.

In 1993, Sakhi organized an international interdisciplinary seminar on the histories of alternative sexualities. This involved both activists and researchers from within and outside India. Most of the papers presented were the result of research carried out in isolation and outside of any academic institution. Researchers living in India spoke of the impossibility of presenting their work even in the more progressive institutional spaces. The content of the seminar covered different historical periods, ranging from the pre-Aryan, Vedic, Puranic, Shaktic, Islamic, etc., to the contemporary contexts. Major attention was paid to gynaefocal and matrilineal traditions. Regional cinemas, various traditions of mythologies and literature, as well as dance forms, were also examined in their construction of gender and sexuality. Activists were encouraged to elaborate on actual experiences, life stories and to exchange personal information.

During the seminar a number of major issues emerged. It was noted that gynaefocal, matrilineal and lesbian histories, which often existed as traditions of the periphery, were being lost at various levels due to the dominance of procreative ideologies at the rural level and the overwhelming construction of any tradition from a solely procreative heterosexual basis. Older alternative mythologies and histories were being manipulated, deformed and mutilated to suit rural male patriarchal ideologies, which led to women being merely the repository of tradition, not its interpreters. This creates rural economies characterized by a gender segregation of labour, an emphasis on boy children as rural capital, and the control of land and economic and cultural resources by men. It also leads to the construction of desire and sexuality from the standpoint of the rural patrilineal male, which is then romanticized by various urban discourses as traditional authenticity. In other words, denial of lesbian sexualities and gynaefocal and matrilineal traditions is perpetuated both from within and outside the rural economies.

Furthermore, with the impact of colonialism dating from the Vedic times, monotheism, orientalism and various forms of nationalism and fundamentalism have all contributed to the destruction of much localized alternative traditions, whether of dance, theatre, literature, visual art, songs or lifestyles. This has ensured the almost complete invisibility of lesbian sexualities. Rather than a pluralistic vision emerging, only procreative and penetrative sexuality is seen as socially acceptable. Traditions expressive of sexual diversity are seen as dirty, deviant and perverted, and the work of evil, over-sexual, devouring women. Very little work has been carried out into the construction of sexuality in general, and in particular, any exploration of lesbian sexualities has become all the more difficult and taboo. No support is given for this work, as it is seen as irrelevant, if not deviant, and therefore undesirable. With the rise of regionalism, fundamentalism and nationalism, much of the localized languages and traditions of alternative sexuality are being lost. The terminology and frameworks are being mutilated to fit into these political expressions, as traditional terms are appropriated and meanings changed.

There is a marked refusal to acknowledge the validity of alternative histories. History as constructed throughout the past represents a uniform and singular perception of a particular world-view. The world-view as expressed in South Asia, has been formed by the central concepts of Vedic Brahmanism, Islam, Christianity and also of Ayurvedic and Western medicalization of the body and sexuality. Male and female roles have been strictly defined and any transgressions of these roles is severely punished by stigmatization, social exclusion, exile, physical abuse and even death. The resultant psycho-social constructions, the denial of different expressions, and the socio-political control of sexualities has resulted in a cultural development that demands compulsory marriage and procreation, that gives no validity and social space for autonomous lesbian women, that demeans unmarried individuals, particularly lesbians, and confers adulthood and thus social status and responsibility on married people. The social pressures to enforce these rules are immense, with the concomitant psychological stresses that such maintenance imposes on the person, the family and the community.

Sexual behaviour takes the place of sexuality. Women's sexual behaviour becomes controlled and marginalized, if not denied. Male sexual behaviour becomes self-absorbed and is reduced to discharge rather than any desire for the other person. Sexual behaviour is depersonalized, the sexual act becoming brutalized, whether between male and female or male and male. There is no social space for any kind of sexuality which is based on women's pleasure or for women who love and desire other women. Concepts of personal choice and privacy become lost, and there can be no development of individuality.

Desires have a history, both personal and social as well as political, in the way they are expressed and manifested. They do not cease to exist as these histories are changed and reformulated; nor do they disappear if such histories are denied or made invisible. But desires are made to fit in with social constructions, and because of the terrible silencing and denial of these histories, a situation of almost total exile has emerged. In trying to resist this exile a closeted and schizophrenic state of being has emerged, where the person tries to assimilate into society through marriage and having children, yet expresses alternative sexual desires in purdah and darkness, shame and silence.

From a questioning of this closeted and schizophrenic state emerged a need to develop culturally relevant and appropriate identities, while resisting the label of being 'Western'. This was the purpose behind the initiation of a project called Jami by the Sakhi network, which still remains the only open lesbian forum. This project represents an excavation into the psycho-erotic histories and cartographies of pleasure and union between women at many levels: sexual, psychical, emotional, mystical, sensual, intellectual, etc., a concept that can best be understood by the earlier notion of *jami*:

> women moving together, with adjacent boundaries,
> sisters, twins [jami] in the expansiveness of the manes;
> they kiss — united, of the [universe's] focal point;
>
> (Rig-Veda 1.85.5, a text older than 1500 BC)

Jami represented a holistic feminine union whereby the *jami* – twins – could be seen as lovers, collective mothers, sisters, companions, etc. The union that is symbolized is neither static nor a complete merger, but rather a coming together, a meeting out of movement. Jami are associated with ideas of togetherness, fusional ecstasy equivalence, diversity in unity, congruence, complementarity, mutuality and reflection.

Sakhi sees itself as questioning the destruction of these traditions, and aims to preserve them through the creation of different kinds of handicrafts using *jami* motifs. This is part of the overall cultural politics of Sakhi. Instead of simplistically using words and concepts developed in the so-called 'first world', it seeks to create other forms of vocabulary that describe erotic bonding between women. Rather than rejecting words such as 'lesbian', the project seeks to enlarge upon their meaning by bringing together different geographic-sexual contexts through language. Thus, when concepts like *sakhi* and *jami* are associated with the word 'lesbian' a multiplicity of contexts are created. Cosmological and philosophical female traditions are grafted onto the sexual political visibility generated by the lesbian movements outside. Moreover, this questions the inherent bigotry of the compartmentalized 'Western' and 'traditional' sides of the modern urban Indian who would not question speaking in English, yet objects to the usage of the word 'lesbian'.

ACKNOWLEDGEMENT

I would like to thank Vilasini for many enlightening discussions.

queering the state: towards a lesbian movement in malaysia

*rais nur and **a.r.***

This article represents an attempt to give a broad picture of the situation facing lesbians in Malaysia, and of factors such as class, religion and ethnicity which impinge on the construction of lesbian identity in Malaysian society. While we believe that it is possible to give a general overview of the situation, we also acknowledge that we are situated, and our perspectives coloured by our particular positions in society – both of us come from middle-class backgrounds and have been educated abroad; one of us is Malay and the other Chinese – and therefore we cannot, and do not purport to, speak for all lesbians in Malaysia. What follows, therefore, is ultimately a personal attempt to identify the issues and challenges faced by lesbians in Malaysia, and to put these often disparate factors and influences into a larger perspective and give them some sort of cohesion.

In order to do this, we propose to first of all provide a brief picture of the Malaysian context in order to enhance the reader's understanding of the interrelated factors that impinge on lesbians here. Then we will define what we mean by the term 'lesbian' and go on to identify and explain the different names used by lesbians in Malaysia to describe themselves or each other. Having given a basic idea of the local scenario, we then describe and assess the impact of socio-legal configurations on lesbian identity and existence. We focus in particular on how women's sexuality generally, and lesbian sexuality specifically, is controlled and regulated by the state and its institutions. Finally, we conclude with our vision for the future, that is, with some ideas on how what we see as largely a bleak situation can be improved in the, we would hope, not too distant future, so that lesbians in Malaysia will achieve increased visibility, representation and autonomy.

Background

The country known as Malaysia today comprises two land masses: East Malaysia, which consists of two states (Sabah and Sarawak) and is situated on the Borneo island, and Peninsular Malaysia, which comprises the remaining eleven states. It has a population of 19 million, half of whom are women. It also has a multi-racial (of which Malays, Chinese and Indians make up the three largest ethnic groups) and multi-religious society, although the official religion is Islam and the national language Bahasa Malaysia.

In recent years, it has joined the ranks of other NICs (newly industrialized countries), boasting an average annual growth rate of over 8 per cent. The nation's economic future is guided by Prime Minister Mahathir bin Mohamad's 'Vision 2020', a thirty-year blueprint launched in 1990 with the aim of establishing Malaysia as a fully developed nation by the year 2020. Part and parcel of this vision, however, has been growing privatization and concentration of capital, which in turn has lead to widening disparities between social groups and between regions.[1]

Although a parliamentary democracy has existed since Independence was declared in 1957, there have never been any serious challenges to the reign of the present ruling party, the National Front, which is an alliance of several political parties. In fact, the opposition is extremely weak in Malaysia, and fails to offer an effective means of 'check and balance' to the government.

Who is a Malaysian lesbian?

We felt it was necessary to give our definition of the term 'lesbian', given the multiplicity of definitions in currency. These range from extremely broad definitions of the word, which include metaphorical[2] (e.g. notions of 'lesbian' as a space or positionality) or emotional dimensions (e.g. a woman whose primary emotional attachments are formed with other women, though she may not necessarily have sex with them), to definitions which are strictly narrow and literal, and which have sexual intimacy between women as their lowest common denominator (i.e. a woman can be called a lesbian only if she has sex with other women, whatever the other dimensions of her relationships with, or the depth of her feelings for, them). However, despite the diversity of meanings of the word 'lesbian', and the rich range of experience it can be said to cover, we believe that our purposes in this essay would best be served by limiting our use of the term to apply to any woman who has sexual relations with other women.

This definition is not unproblematic, as such a narrow definition necessarily excludes many people who consider themselves lesbian but do not practise lesbian sex, such as lesbian celibates or other women-identified women. In fact, early on in our research, we wanted to include women who identified themselves as lesbian as part of our definition, and therefore hinge our definition on the self-identification of the woman concerned. This, however, became untenable, because as we progressed we came across many women who have sexual relations with women but do not the use the word 'lesbian' to describe themselves. For some of these women, such a word was alien to them, and in some cases they were hardly aware that other lesbians existed. Others were familiar with the concept of homosexuality, but used words other than 'lesbian' to identify themselves. Thus we decided that our use of the term would refer to women who have sexual relations with other women, regardless of whether or not they use the word to describe themselves.

Our knowledge is primarily of urban and middle-class lesbians, although we have made attempts to access the experiences of others. Lesbianism is a phenomenon which exists very much underground, in the sense that there is very little public discourse about it (and what little there is frequently pathologizes it) and very few safe spaces in which lesbians can be out or come together to share their experiences. Furthermore, the experience of being a lesbian in Malaysia is heavily influenced by ethnicity and class. These two factors make it difficult to extract an account of lesbian experience which can address lesbian existence in both urban as well as rural areas, and apply across class and ethnic divides.

Unlike gay men, who have been united through work against HIV/AIDS, there has been no similar phenomenon which has sparked this move towards a sense of community for lesbians, so that by and large there are many tight-knit groups, based on race or class, which do not intermingle with each other: Malay lesbians generally have a different network and socialize at different places from Chinese and Indians, working class from middle class, urban from rural, etc.

The players

In as far as it is possible to generalize, one aspect which can be said to be common to all these different subcultures is role-playing, or the construction of lesbian identity around notions of the 'butch' and the 'femme', with their attendant 'masculine' and 'feminine' traits. While Western countries like the UK and the USA have recently seen a resurgence of the butch and the femme in lesbian culture, this has mainly been dictated by fashion and the 'lesbian chic' trend, which in the UK saw many straight women dressing like dykes and lesbian characters suddenly appearing in various soap operas, and partly by postmodern notions of parody, irony and 'genderfuck'. That is to say, while some lesbians do take butch/femme roles seriously in these countries, many others see adopting these roles as a fashionable thing to do and/or a way of subverting essentialist notions of sex and gender, and parodying notions of identity/sexuality as stable and immutable rather than fluid and constantly changing. So a lesbian who dresses as a butch one day may very well decide to dress as a femme the next, and vice versa.

In Malaysia though, butch/femme roles are taken very seriously by the majority of lesbians, and there is no element of playfulness or parody to them. The word 'butch', though generally used to refer to a lesbian who adopts or exhibits traits and behaviour socially deemed to be masculine, in fact covers a continuum of identifications or definitions. At the lower end of the scale is the 'tomboy' who dresses in a boyish manner, generally looks like a cute boy, and yet it is still possible to tell that she is female. The tomboy figures in all cultures.

'Peng-kids' occupy the middle of the continuum, and are generally associated with Malay working-class lesbians. The word 'peng-kid' is derived from 'punk kid', as they are deemed to have borrowed heavily from punk culture in terms of their attire. Peng-kids often feel that they are men trapped in women's bodies. They bind their breasts as well as use men's underwear and aftershave. They are renowned as very loyal and extremely attentive and generous to their girlfriends. The peng-kid phenomenon, which can be traced back to the 1970s, is now very widespread and exists in both rural and urban Malay communities. The term has also been adopted among some Chinese lesbians, who abbreviate it to 'PK'.

Finally, there are the 'hardcore' butches. In the West, what is known as a 'bulldyke' or 'bulldagger' would be the closest equivalents to the local hardcore. Whereas peng-kids feel that they are men trapped in women's bodies, and thereby acknowledge their femaleness to some degree, in many cases, these hardcore butches do not even perceive themselves as women, and pass as men whenever possible. Many consider the idea of sex-change operations seriously at some stage in their lives. Hardcores exist in all cultures in Malaysian society, but appear to be predominantly working class.

Butch identifications in Malaysia are therefore multiple and complex. Things become simpler when we come to femme identity. Generally, femmes are perceived to be straight women in disguise, or women who, although they might be involved in a lesbian relationship, have the option to 'become normal' and conduct relationships with men. A femme's lesbianism is therefore not seen as essential or fixed; whereas butches see themselves, and are perceived, as having no choice about their sexuality – they are definitely and incontrovertibly lesbian. Many femmes have lesbian relationships in order to avoid the complications of becoming pregnant, which might happen in heterosexual relationships. Another reason why femmes prefer butches to men is that they believe they are more secure in a relationship with a butch, since it is not as easy for butches to abandon one woman for another as it is for men, given the relatively small lesbian subcultures which exist in Malaysia.

In many senses, this emphasis on roles is very restrictive, and those who resist defining themselves in such a way often find that they are treated with distrust and hostility by their peers, as are lesbians who change identifications. There is some degree of policing within the lesbian communities in Malaysia, and what is acceptable in terms of clothing and appearance, sexual practices and roles is clearly defined and strictly enforced. This means that lesbians who reject such pressures and constructions of identity are excluded. More importantly, in their insistence on butch/femme identifications such lesbians reinforce the stereotypical notions of lesbians and lesbianism harboured by society at large, rather than challenging them or presenting alternative constructions of identity, alternative ways of being lesbian.

Partly, this dependence on roles has to do with the fact that lesbians feel beleaguered by the homophobia and hostility of society as a whole, and therefore do not trust people easily – choosing a role and sticking with it signifies a willingness to belong, to play by the rules, and indicates that one is an 'insider' rather than an 'outsider' and therefore can be trusted. But we feel it is also partly to do with the lack of any political dimension to lesbianism in Malaysia, restricting it solely to the sexual dimension.

Lesbians in the West have played a prominent role within feminist campaigning since the 1960s, and have contributed greatly to, and learned a lot from, feminism and its insights. Lesbian and queer theory, as it exists in the West today, has its roots in the feminist movement, and has built upon feminism's interrogation of the categories of gender, its assertion, for example, that, as Simone de Beauvoir put it, 'one is not born a woman, one becomes one'. 'Masculinity' and 'femininity' were shown to be states of being which were socially constructed and therefore avoidable, rather than biological and inevitable.

While, on the one hand, many feminists made the political decision to become lesbians in the light of feminism's analyses of gender relations, and as a logical extension of their politics, on the other, many lesbians used and extended the analytical foundations laid down by feminism to challenge and deconstruct the institution of heterosexuality – to expose it as an instrument of patriarchy or, at any rate, something which is neither more natural nor more inevitable than any other sexual preference or tendency. Lesbian feminists, in line with the early feminist tenet that 'the personal is political' therefore identified the realm of sexuality and sexual practices as the locus of much patriarchal power and oppression, and proceeded to problematize heterosexuality and politicize lesbianism, arguing that it represented a subversive force in its refusal to fall in with dominant/patriarchal concepts of what is natural or permissible in society.

This perception of lesbianism as having a political dimension rather than simply a sexual one, of being not simply something restricted and limited to the bedroom, but having wider implications and political resonances, is, however, largely absent in Malaysia. There is very little sense (or perceived need) here that lesbianism is or can be a political force, or that it can be used to critique or challenge dominant patriarchal and heterosexual ideologies and institutions. We believe that this has to do with the fact that feminism, which is closely connected with the lesbian movement in the West, has not translated well here, nor has it had the impact which it had in the West. As a newly industrializing country, Malaysia faces different challenges and has different priorities to that of 'first world' or Western countries, and often feminism is not perceived to be, or made relevant to, the needs and lives of women here.

At any rate, without feminism's insights on how patriarchy works to oppress women and how gender roles function to reinforce patriarchal power, many lesbians simply adopt heterosexual notions of gender and replicate heterosexual relationships without questioning or problematizing them. It may, of course, be argued that these lesbians adopt butch/femme roles as a conscious eroticization of difference.[3] But we believe that it is rather a case of a lack of alternatives. The invisibilizing of lesbians in society, and the lack of role models who practise alternative ways of defining themselves or conducting relationships, of course reinforces the above.

All this – the invisibilizing of lesbians in society, the lack of a political dimension to lesbianism and of emancipatory movements such as feminism or a gay movement – fits into the larger context of the repressive and authoritarian nature of the state. We will now go on, therefore, to examine the extent to which the state and its institutions or silencing mechanisms repress and inhibit lesbians, and thus impede the growth of a national lesbian movement.

The Malaysian state

While the image it promotes suggests otherwise, the reality of the Malaysian political system is that it is extremely repressive. There is a litany of laws which serves to restrict civil liberties.[4] Thus, although there has never been a police state (except briefly when the Emergency was declared in 1969 and Parliament was suspended for a few months), or a military presence as experienced by the neighbouring countries of the Philippines, Thailand and Indonesia, there is a deep-seated fear of authority which is enough to keep all citizens in check, but even more those who are perceived as morally deviant.

PLAYING WITH FIRE: LESBIANS AND THE LAW

Many people are under the impression that homosexuality is illegal in Malaysia. However, there is no actual law against it.[5] The law is silent on this matter. In 1994, for example, operators of discos and nightspots in Kuala Lumpur were warned by the local City Hall Licensing Department Director not to 'discriminate against customers who were "tomboys" or gays since the law was silent on them … '. She made the remark in response to an incident in which a popular disco denied entry to a young woman with short-cropped hair on the pretext that the management did not allow 'tomboys' into the club.[6] Another City Hall advisory board member added that 'it was also discrimination to bar gays in the club, so long as they did not conduct themselves in an unruly manner'.[7]

Although the law does not specifically prohibit homosexuality, it does however prohibit acts that may be construed as homosexual behaviour. For example, Section 377 of the Penal Code refers to 'Unnatural Offences' and Section 377A prohibits 'carnal intercourse against the order of nature'. Under this law, 'any person who has sexual connection with another person by the introduction of the penis into the anus or mouth of the other person is said to commit carnal intercourse against the order of nature'.[8] Clearly, this law is not applicable to lesbians, and it has never even been used against two consenting adult males. It has, however, been utilized in conjunction with cases of sexual assault involving an adult male offender and a (male) minor.

There are other provisions under the law which may be used against lesbians and gay men. Several pieces of legislation in the Penal Code, Minor Offences Act and the Women and Girls Protection Act could be used against lesbians for behaviour that offends public morals or righteousness. For example, Section 377D ('Outrages on Decency') of the Penal Code states that:

> Any person who, in public or private, commits, or abets the commission of, or procures or attempts to procure the commission by any person, of any act of gross indecency with another person, shall be punished with imprisonment for a term which may extend to two years.[9]

For now, it would seem that if these laws were to be used against lesbians, it would be more for the purposes of harassment than conviction. Like transsexuals,[10] lesbians are not perceived as a threat but rather as a 'public nuisance'. As there have been no test cases of this nature, it is difficult to gauge how effective these laws would be. And it appears that for this specific law to be used to penalize lesbians, the court would first of all have to prove that lesbian sex constitutes an act of 'gross indecency'.

Censorship laws which allow the state to ban and confiscate materials it deems offensive also pose a threat to lesbians. It is illegal to distribute or even have in one's possession any 'obscene' materials (books, magazines, etc.). Offenders are liable to face sentences of up to a maximum of three years' imprisonment, be fined, or both.[11]

While the following scenario is hypothetical, it gives an idea of the threat this law poses to lesbians. A group of women goes away for a weekend holiday. They rent a bungalow which has a caretaker. The caretaker gets suspicious when he sees these women partnering off into their bedrooms at the end of the day. His suspicions lead him to call the police. The police come to the premises on the pretext that there is intention to commit an unlawful act. They enter the rooms, discover lesbian materials and charge the women for possession of obscene materials.

While it is up to the court to define what is obscene, in all likelihood lesbian-related material will be deemed as such. We are aware of instances in which videos of lesbian films such as *Go Fish* and *Desert Hearts* have been seized by customs; and safer-sex videos would definitely receive similar treatment.

Any discussion around legal dangers confronting lesbians in Malaysia would not be complete without mention of the Internal Security Act (ISA). Essentially, the ISA gives the state the right to detain anyone it perceives as being a threat to national security. It has been used arbitrarily by the state ever since its enactment in 1960. In 1987, over one hundred people were detained under the ISA, including politicians, social activists, church activists, trade unionists, academics, educationists, women's and human rights activists. Given the all-encompassing scope of this Act and the state's stand on moral righteousness, it is probable that it will use the ISA against homosexuals if and when the need arises.

The above examples are relevant in the context of the civil/criminal law system. There is also a separate set of laws governing Muslims in the country. Known as Syariah laws (which are Islamic religious laws),[12] their implementation is confined to family administration and particular criminal offences. It is difficult to ascertain what the Syariah laws say about homosexuality, because the subject is not widely known among lay people. However, it would be fair to say that many perceive homosexuality to be un-Islamic.

In 1993, the state of Kelantan enacted the Syariah Criminal Code (II) – otherwise known as the Hudud laws (Islamic penal laws).[13] Under these laws, 'the act of sexual gratification between females by rubbing the vagina of one against that of the other'[14] was made an offence. Punishment is to be meted out according to the discretion of the judge. Fortunately, the enforcement of the Hudud laws has been stalled by the federal government's rejection of them – at least for the time being.

Although no lesbian in Malaysia has been prosecuted under existing laws – civil/criminal or Syariah – one cannot imagine a lesbian making a public declaration of her sexuality without some form of backlash. The sentiments expressed by the City Hall officials are an exception rather than the norm. In a country where the general public does not have much knowledge of the law and of what is legal or not, prejudice against homosexuals can easily combine with public hysteria to add to the general confusion.

PUBLIC DISCOURSES AND THE REGULATION OF WOMEN'S SEXUALITY

As the country pushes towards Vision 2020, rapid industrialization and unchecked growth has not only resulted in the marginalization of certain quarters but a rise in disturbing social phenomena on a scale previously unparalleled. For example, there have been more reportings of domestic violence, rising numbers of unwed mothers and single women, increasing incidents of missing (and trafficking in) women, as well as growing numbers of young Malaysians 'loafing' in public areas.[15]

The state's most convenient excuse has been to blame these social 'ills' on growing moral decay, which has in turn been linked to the importation of Western values.[16] Western values, argued government ministers, have no place in Malaysia, and would lead to the destruction of the family unit. According to the Prime Minister:

> We want a family unit to remain, that is, having a husband and a wife and their children ... not a man being married to another man or a woman and a woman, or single parenthood. We do not accept such means of unlimited freedom.[17]

Citing the need to uphold Asian family values, the Ministry of Information has also been able to ban gays and transvestites from appearing on TV. The message was clear: 'We do not want to encourage any form of homosexuality in our society.'[18] Thus, under the banner of protecting Asian values, the state has been able systematically to attack those it perceives as moral dangers to society. Women, especially young women, have borne the brunt of these attacks. The following examples illustrate this point.

In September 1994, a local newspaper highlighted the emergence of a group of young women known as *boh sia*.[19] These women would allegedly hang out in public places and engage in casual sex with men who picked them up – in other words, these were 'promiscuous' women. State reaction was swift. Using the Women and Girls Protection Act 1973, police randomly rounded up these young women (including those who frequented shopping complexes/malls) in the name of protecting them. The imposition of curfews was also proposed.

Another incident involved the then Chief Minister of Malacca,[20] who was accused of being sexually involved with a sixteen-year old minor. Normally this would be classified as statutory rape. However, despite acknowledging that there were 'strong suspicions', the Attorney General announced that the case had to be dropped as there was insufficient evidence for it to be brought to court.[21] While the minister was allowed to get away scot-free, the sixteen-year-old was put under police custody and later sent to a rehabilitation centre under the Women and Girls Protection Act! A deputy minister in the Prime Minister's department went further, and advocated that she be prosecuted under Islamic laws for having illicit sex and becoming pregnant out of wedlock.[22] Thus, instead of penalizing the ex-Chief Minister for gross abuse of powers, the state justified punitive action against the young woman on grounds of her immorality.

Both incidents illustrate just how women's sexuality can be controlled and regulated by direct state intervention. However, it is important to note that the (conservative) discourses which underpin the state and its institutions function at all levels of society. So, even when the state does not intervene, women's sexuality can be policed by 'the moral majority' through an appeal to these values and beliefs. In 1994, for instance, a Kuala Lumpur-based women's organization produced a booklet entitled *Lina's Dilemma* which dealt with the issue of young women and HIV/AIDS. During a public exhibition when the booklet was distributed, it fell into the hands of a local tabloid paper, which subsequently featured the booklet on its front cover under the heading of 'Risalah Biadab' ('Offensive Booklet'). Among other things, the newspaper alleged that *Lina's Dilemma* was more pornographic than a blue movie, and that it advocated free sex.[23] Public opinion varied from perceiving the contents as anti-Islamic to merely culturally inappropriate. No one, however, came out in defence of the booklet.

This incident demonstrates the difficulty in addressing the issue of sex and sexuality in Malaysian society. Yet the cultural sanctions against raising young women's awareness of issues to do with sex can cost these women their lives, especially in the face of the HIV/AIDS epidemic. Keeping young women in ignorance and denying them knowledge of their bodies and safer sex therefore exacts a price which we believe is far too high to pay for not offending cultural sensitivities.

'Somewhere over the rainbow': opportunities and options for the future

Although the situation facing lesbians in Malaysia can be described as extremely oppressive, we believe that a potential for change does exist, and we would now like to identify some spaces or entities which we see as representing such a potential.

THE WOMEN'S MOVEMENT

The range of women's organizations in Malaysia – from the ultra-conservatives to the more open and liberal-minded – makes it difficult to discern what level of acceptance the issue of lesbianism has within the women's movement. Suffice to say, none have come out in support of lesbian rights. This is not altogether surprising since even on subjects such as feminism, the more progressive groups do not make public their stand. Perhaps because lesbians have drawn very little attention to themselves, conservative and morally righteous English-speaking urbanites react against feminism instead. The point here is that if such groups are unable to take a public position on feminism, what more can they do on something as contentious as lesbianism?

The fear of being discredited – rightly or wrongly – is very real among women's groups, especially the more progressive ones which provide alternative points of view. Often, any action has to be taken with one eye on the dominant 'cultural sensitivities' of the population. The incident involving the publication of *Lina's Dilemma*, not only demonstrates societal attitudes about sex and sexuality but also the differences among women's groups on such issues. Given that some of the criticisms came from within the women's movement itself, this incident also displays the difficulties any women's group would face if it were to contemplate raising the issue of sexuality, let alone lesbian rights.

When asked why the women's movement did not address the issue of lesbianism, the response given by a local feminist activist was that 'Lesbians in Malaysia have to organize and make their voices heard. They need to form some sort of pressure group. It is not in the interest of women who are not lesbians to push this issue.' But a lesbian pressure group will only come about if lesbians believe that there will be some degree of support forthcoming from such women's groups. What appears as a chicken-and-egg situation would not be so if public censure was not viewed as a threat. It would also appear that anti-lesbianism in the women's movement has contributed to the failure to make the necessary connections between lesbian rights and women's rights.

While the seeds for a progresssive feminist movement have been planted, it appears that it will take some time yet for a situation to arise where lesbian rights can be placed alongside other issues on the movement's agenda. Needless to say, so long as women's groups continue to ignore the lesbian question, they are reinforcing the ongoing invisibility of lesbians, thus impeding the formation of a lesbian movement.

A HOMOSEXUAL MOVEMENT: THE ROLE OF LESBIAN AND GAY GROUPS

Ironically, the tragedy of HIV/AIDS has offered some scope for mobilizing the homosexual community in Malaysia. Recognizing that it was unable to single-handedly deal with the epidemic, the government turned to other non-governmental organizations (NGOs) for assistance in combating the spread of HIV/AIDS. One of the groups which responded to this call was Pink Triangle (PT). Although PT is known as an organization working with gay men, through its HIV/AIDS work it has quickly become an acceptable organization whose gay element has been overlooked by the state,[24] in particular the Health Ministry. Becoming more visible and credible has thus created new opportunities to build solidarity between lesbians and gay men.

PT now serves as a centre where lesbians and gay men can come together. Although its members are predominantly male, PT has always been open to women. As such, it offers a space for lesbians to be visible and safe. Thus far, lesbians and gay men have not intermingled much. This was partly because lesbians felt alienated by the sexism within the gay male community, but it was also due to the lack of a common cause. Now, at least, there is some possibility for them to come together and unite in their concern about HIV/AIDS. This, in the view of local gay male activists, is essential for building a solidarity which will enhance our chances of survival.[25] It may even form the beginnings of a lesbian and gay movement. In fact, knowing that an organization for gay men existed assisted in the formation of a lesbian group in 1992. Even though the group has not 'come-out' publicly as a lesbian organization, it is becoming increasingly known among the local lesbian community, particularly among Chinese lesbians. Having spent the earlier days grappling with direction and objectives, the group presently emphasizes community-building and the empowerment of lesbians, and has had initial success in linking different lesbian interests together.

Conclusion

Of course, while there are such opportunities, there are also questions to consider. Will feminism ever take off in Malaysia and provide the impetus for a lesbian movement? What will it take for women's groups to support lesbian rights? Will lesbians ever feel comfortable in a gay space provided by PT? Will it ever be as chic to know about (and support) a lesbian event in the same way as it is to hang out at and support gay events?[26] How long will PT be tolerated before conservative forces retaliate? Such questions should not be viewed as wholly negative. Instead, they should be seen as challenges which must be addressed in the interests of strengthening and promoting a viable lesbian and gay rights movement. Similarly, while we may have painted a discouraging picture of the situation facing lesbians in Malaysia as a whole, this was due to our desire to accurately reflect the reality of what it means to be a lesbian here, rather than to a defeatist or pessimistic outlook. Ultimately, what is crucial is our desire for and commitment to change.

ACKNOWLEDGEMENTS

The authors would like to thank everyone who contributed their experiences to this essay. Due to fears of repercussions, it is not possible to name them.

NOTES

1. Johan Saravanamuttu *et al.* 'The pitfalls of NICdom' in *Asian Exchange* vol. 8, no. 1–2 (1992).
2. Literary theorists and postmodern critics, especially, have invested in concepts of the lesbian as metaphor or as existing at another level than the material. Recent examples of such a trend include Elizabeth Meese, *(Sem)erotics: Theorizing Lesbian Writing* (New York: New York University Press, 1992), and Karla Jay and Joanne Glasgow (eds) *Lesbian Texts and Contexts: Radical Revisions* (New York: New York University Press, 1990). This has in part been influenced by the rise of post-structuralist discourses which have problematized traditional concepts of identity and epistemology.

3. See Susan Ardill and Sue O'Sullivan, 'Butch/Femme Obsessions', *Feminist Review* 34 (Spring, 1990), pp. 79–85, for a highly lucid and ingenious theory on the erotics of difference underlying butch and femme identifications.
4. Johan Saravanamutta *et al. op. cit.* These laws include the Internal Security Act, Seditions Act, Official Secrets Act, Printing Act, Broadcasting Act and the Societies Act.
5. This applies to both lesbians and gay men.
6. *New Straits Times*, 25 August 1994. She also said that 'every member of the public who is of legal age had the right to patronize nightspots so long as they were decently dressed and did not misbehave'.
7. *Ibid.*
8. Legal Research Board (compiled by), Penal Code (FMS Cap. 45), International Law Book Services, Kuala Lumpur. Under the original Section 377, there had only been a few prosecutions, which suggests that it did not need to be amended. In fact, the amendments were an indirect result of women's groups' efforts to reform the Laws Relating to Rape (under the Penal Code) in 1989.
9. *Ibid.*
10. In recent round-ups of transsexuals, police have openly stated that their actions are conducted to harass transsexuals off the streets.
11. Penal Code (FMS Cap. 45), Section 292–293.
12. Syariah laws vary from state to state, given that Islamic matters in each state are regulated by their own enactments.
13. Legally, this refers to a punishment which has been prescribed by God in the revealed text of the Qur'an or the Sunnah. Rose Ismail (ed.) *Hudud in Malaysia: The Issues at Stake* (Kuala Lumpur: Sisters in Islam 1995).
14. *Ibid.*
15. Loafing among youths is commonly known as *lepak*. The state has been extremely concerned that it will lead to a degeneration of young Malaysians who were expected to carry on Vision 2020, thus jeopardizing the nation's future success. In response to *lepak*, a whole institution called *Rakan Muda* (Friend of Youth) has been created to prepare young Malaysians to face nation-building challenges. It consists of twelve state-endorsed programmes, e.g. sports, martial arts, community work, religion, etc.
16. For most of 1994, the Prime Minister and other government ministers conducted a tirade against Western values, associating them with

immorality. Ironically, Western influence has increased with the liberalization of the Malaysian economy under Vision 2020. It was not until 1995 that the Prime Minister conceded that not all Asian values were good and not all Western values bad. See *The Star*, 15 March 1995.

17. *The Star*, 11 September 1994.
18. The Minister of Information, as quoted in *The Star*, 7 August 1994.
19. *New Straits Times*, 16 September 1994.
20. One of the four Malaysian states which do not have a Sultan as head of government.
21. *The Star*, 22 October 1994.
22. *Ibid*.
23. *Harian Metro*, 24 August 1994. On 25 August, another three articles related to the booklet appeared. In actual fact, the accusations hurled were probably in relation to the mention of kissing, licking and massaging, as well as a clinical diagram on how to use a condom. However, by 27 August, the incident was reduced to a comic clipping and finally, after the organization wrote in to protest about the inaccurate reportage, the newspaper reprinted parts of the letter on 3 September.
24. As illustrated throughout this article, the gay community is still subjected to attacks from other quarters of the state. An incident several years ago at a local gay bar saw hundreds of gay men rounded up and kept at the police station overnight, on the pretext of having their urine tested for drugs. More disturbing, however, was the presence of the press during the round-up and the repercussions that followed after photos of the incident, and references made to the gay bar, were published the next day.
25. Interview with two Pink Triangle activists.
26. PT has held two successful HIV/AIDS cabarets which had gay (including drag queen) performers. Both attracted crowds, including Kuala Lumpur's rich and famous. While gay venues are thriving, the only known lesbian space for middle-class Kuala Lumpur lesbians was closed (by the proprietors) within a year of opening, on the pretext of making the space more exclusive for upper middle-class lesbians.

5 indonesian lesbians writing their own script: issues of feminism and sexuality

b.j.d. gayatri

Feminism is a concept that is strictly Western and unsuitable for Indonesian women, an expert argues. 'Indonesian women have their own concepts and strategies inspired by their own religious, cultural and traditional values', R. A. Tity Koesomodardo said in a seminar. The lifestyles of Western women stress individualism, said Tity, who was formerly one of Indonesia's officials in the United Nations and in Europe. In the Indonesian ideology, 'independence' has nothing to do with individualism, and local women are bound to their natural obligations, such as raising children. (*Jakarta Post*, 2 May 1995)

I can understand that transsexuals experience mental and psychological suffering, so that society can accept them. I can also understand that lesbians have individual rights, but I cannot accept them as Indonesian women. My belief is that lesbianism is not in accordance with Pancasila [Indonesia's five-point state ideology], because lesbians have forgotten their fundamental duties to be mothers, giving birth and raising children . . . . (statement by Mien Sugandhi, Minister for Women's Affairs, *Suara Karya*, 6 June 1994)

When I was asked to write this article, despite feeling pressurised by the limited time available, I was anxious to make the most of the opportunity since so little has been written about Indonesia. My experience overseas has been that people have no understanding of Indonesia or the situation of women here. While it is true to say that the Dutch (ex-colonial power) display some awareness, this is certainly not the case in the rest of Europe, and in North and South America. At best, people have heard of Bali as a paradise island belonging to Indonesia. In brief, Indonesia is the world's biggest archipelago, with a population of approximately 187 million according to the 1992 census (now 195.6 million: *Kompas*, 18 August 1995). It is the fourth biggest nation after China, India and the USA.

Indonesian culture is made up of about 330 ethnic groups with 707 languages, with Bahasa Indonesia employed as the national lingua franca.[1] The Javanese majority means that its culture is dominant and that most government officials are also Javanese.[2]

This article aims to provide an overview of feminism and its relationship to female homosexuality, and will show how in the Indonesian women's movement the issue of sexuality, particularly female homosexuality, is commonly excluded both at the philosophical level and in their activities. Another important issue I address is the significant influence of the mass media on the interpretation of feminist ideas, and the way in which it deals with female homosexuality. I place particular emphasis on the influence of the media in forming public opinion and furthering stereotypical views of women.

The women's movement and feminism

A discussion of the women's movement in Indonesia must start with an understanding of the difference between the women's groups formed under the Old Order, or during the period of Indonesia's independence struggle, and those groups that appeared under the New Order, particularly in the 1980s.[3] During the independence struggle at the end of the 1920s, and before independence in 1945, an awareness of women's emancipation already existed but was sidelined by the primary concern of achieving national independence. After independence the issue of women's emancipation was rediscovered, and appears in the 1945 constitution (Undang-undang Dasar Republik Indonesia 1945), which is based on principles of egalitarianism and gender parity, as well as in the marriage laws, which were prepared after 1950 and formalized in 1974.[4]

In the 1980s new women's organizations appeared, primarily in the form of NGOs (non-governmental organisations), espousing feminist philosophy. The hotly debated issues in Europe and the USA were central to these groups, but tended to be ineffectual as they were not based in existing local problems.[5] This partly relates to the accusation from the media and the elder generation that Western approaches are not appropriate for Eastern culture. Personally I disagree with the term 'Western', as it has various meanings for Indonesians, however at this point I am using it to refer to the popular Indonesian understanding of non-Eastern/Asian culture as evidenced in the Jakarta press clippings at the beginning of this article.

At present both the print and electronic media frequently maintain that feminism has no place in Indonesian culture. Indeed, they go so far as to generalize that feminism is not part of Eastern culture, in order to justify the statement about Indonesia and thus close off the possibilities of evaluating the meaning of feminism for Indonesian women, while condemning those who try to do so with the charge of importing inappropriate 'Western culture'. This statement has also often been used by government bureaucrats and some of the previous generation of women activists, who have been following the government line and attacking other women activists for using a feminist framework. These women are accused of forgetting their roots and culture, as feminism is perceived to be inappropriate because its origins lie in Western thought. Ironically, in many other fields Indonesia is importing Western technology wholesale in the interests of development and modernization: for example, TV and aspects of the physical infrastructure such as apartments and shopping malls. An example from daily life is the intrusion of American junk food such as Kentucky Fried Chicken, Pizza Hut and McDonald's, which, while clearly alien to Indonesian culture, is not only accepted but admired as modern food.

Since 1978 the government has used a programme for women, particularly lower-class women, which ties them to the responsibilities of 'prosperous family education' and ensures that they are confined to the domestic sphere. Women married to civil servants must participate in the Dharma Wanita programme.[6] These two programmes have been the target of criticism from the 1980s generation of women's groups because of their influence in tying women to traditional functions, such as raising children and supporting the husband, while taking a subordinate position. Meanwhile, women's organizations of the earlier generation are involved in supporting these programmes, and accuse the feminist-influenced groups of forgetting their female destiny and cultural roots by taking on Western thought and lifestyle.

Such accusations of Westernism make it hard to raise popular awareness that the issue is not one of East and West but of women's issues, which can arise anywhere. An example of the difficulty of raising women's issues as opposed to development issues, is the question of rape. This was first raised in 1990 by various women's organizations established in the mid-1980s (the earlier generation of women's organizations said the rape issue was inappropriate (because 'feminist'), overstated and invented). Nevertheless, by the end of July 1995, rape had become an important issue in the national newspapers, with many readers sending letters supporting heavier sentences (*Kompas* 26 July–7 August 1995). The Minister for Women's Affairs herself expressed the opinion that rapists should be sentenced to death (*Kompas* 28 July 1995). Thus, it has taken five years for the mass media to accept the seriousness of rape and to accede to the demand that rapists should receive heavier sentences (prior to this the maximum had been seven years).

The rape controversy also illustrates the difficulty of bringing a women's issue which is central to Indonesian society to the attention of the authorities. Even more difficult is the relationship between women and religion, since the majority of Indonesian women are Muslim and are expected to accept the dogmatic view of women's relationship to men propagated by male religious leaders. Furthermore, the treatment of reproductive health and contraception in the family-planning programme has also disadvantaged women, with the adoption of Western technology, without due regard to the side-effects, by a government obsessed with controlling population growth. Women who protest or criticize this programme are held to be obstructing government policy, which is one aspect of the dilemma of the women's movement in Indonesia. As I have shown, opposition to feminism comes not only from men, but also from other women.

To some extent the issues faced are universal, yet the ideas are consistently held to have arisen in the West, and so the accusation 'not part of Indonesian culture' can be applied. This accusation is also levelled at lesbians and gay men. I shall refer to the former as 'female homosexuals' since, in view of the negative image presented of lesbian life the term 'lesbian' has been rejected by many Indonesian non-heterosexual women I have encountered.[7]

Feminism, female homosexuality and sexuality

Various factors need to be considered in order to understand the issue of female homosexuality in Indonesia. Firstly, there is the influence of culture, which varies according to the woman's family background. Secondly, there is the understanding of homosexuality as it is interpreted by 'culture' and as it is established in public opinion through the mass media. Thirdly, gender and sexuality studies have emerged as a significant area of academic thought in Europe, the USA and Australia, and are now exerting an influence on the Indonesian women's movement, although needless to say the ideas are interpreted somewhat differently. The discourse on sexuality is in its earliest stages, and many people are still afraid to discuss it or remain confused by the level of abstraction required. The Indonesian discourse continually comes back to heterosexuality, while still applying Freudian theories that are fifty years out of date.

In Indonesia, homosexuality is seen as a lifestyle that is taken up by the urban youth who want to be thought trendy. The impression conveyed by the print media is that the stereotypical life of the female homosexual is part of a world of criminality, drugs, nightlife, promiscuity and sickness. While this is undboutedly a part of urban life, caused primarily by women's difficulty in finding work, previous research and current realities also show that homosexuality has a traditional place in Indonesian society. Many psychologists and scientists still maintain that homosexuality is an abnormality which can be cured, while religious leaders and government officials instruct the public to avoid such deviant behaviour and fulfil their obligations to marry and have children.[8]

The acceptance of the idea of the 'third sex' in Indonesia is clear from the writing of Gilbert Herdt on Irian and various other studies sent to Indonesia's national gay bulletin *Gaya Nasantara*.[9] Indonesian society is more familiar with male homosexuals and transsexuals, which is not surprising given the worldwide phenomenon of men in the public sphere and the belief that they create the culture. However, my own historical research has shown that female sexuality also occupies a traditional place in Indonesia, specifically in Java. But because women are always perceived to be in a domestic role within Javanese social structure, this phenomenon has never been acknowledged, while female homosexuals themselves have tried to exist in the female sphere without being exposed as a social phenomenon.[10] This gives women little opportunity to be open about their lives including their sexual lives, and thus it is not surprising that female homosexuality is ignored.

Meanwhile, the debate over the role of female homosexuals/lesbians[11] in the feminist movement is always a hot topic. It became particularly heated in the lead up to the Fourth United Nations World Conference on Women in Beijing. Among the matters raised at the conference, such as women's rights and violence against women, the issue of sexuality was promoted by international lesbian groups as being intrinsic to feminism. The problem in Indonesia is that feminism is only understood in relation to the stereotypical portrayal of the women's liberation movement that is continually presented in the media. Women's groups using feminist ideas are frequently labelled lesbian, with the result that they try and distance themselves from the issue of female homosexuality or related issues of sexuality. While in the context of national or international workshops or meetings, women activists may be supportive, this is not the case in daily life, by which I mean the way they deal with female homosexuals; something that has been part of my own experience.

Several years ago I went through a process of searching for my sexuality and questioning the heterosexist patriarchy, with the result that I became open about my sexuality and moved in with my girlfriend. For various reasons I did not discuss this with my friends in the women's movement, until a close friend questioned me about my private life. In a very short time the news that I was living with another woman became the subject of gossip among Jakarta women activists. I felt that I had been 'outed' without concern for my state of mind or my social situation, which led to a nightmare lasting several months. Many female homosexuals avoid the women's movement because they do not want to go through this experience, and at the same time they feel that the issue of their sexuality is a private one which is not related to the current state of feminist discourse in Indonesia.

At this point I need to explain that the Indonesian government maintains a tight control over sexuality.[12] The institution of marriage is the only approved context for sexual relations, outside of which sex is only practised by men and prostitutes.[13] Almost three years ago myself and a group of friends set up a group to study sexuality, and I was pushed by the others to discuss the importance of sexuality for women. In the following discussion the female activists/feminists who attended asked about the technical aspects of sexual relations. Up to that point I was not aware that I had become the Indonesian 'Sexpert'; it was well before I read Susie Bright's book![14] Suddenly one of my friends naively said, 'Gayatri how come you talk about sex but you are not married yet?' which left me momentarily speechless.

Further understanding of female homosexuality is also limited by the stereotype of butch and femme roles, which is evident among women's activists from both the pre-New Order period and the 1980s. To give an example, I remember an incident that occurred at a national meeting of women's NGOs in Jakarta, prior to the Jakarta Ministerial Meeting in 1994 (one of the pre-conference meetings for the Beijing conference), which I attended as a representative of Indonesian female homosexuals. I wore my usual clothes, except for a headband instead of my more familiar hairclips. Some of the women knew me as a female homosexual but not as the organizer, so they were surprised when I registered myself as a representative of ALN-Indonesia.[15] There was also suprise that the meeting should be attended by a representative of female homosexuals.

During the meeting, friends whispered that I was the object of gossip, not because of my links with the ALN or other Asian groups, but because, 'although she is a lesbian, she is feminine'. This surprised me as I was wearing trousers like many others, but I happened to have picked a pink shirt. Since many other women were wearing skirts or even Muslim jilbab, I am not sure what they meant by 'feminine'. According to my friends, the women's perception of female homosexuals is that they must be butch-looking. I did not think my appearance was either butch or femme, but the issue always seems to arise in the Asian women's movement. At the regional NGO meeting in Manila a couple of months earlier, lesbian[16] representatives demanded that they should not be discriminated against on the basis of dress, or be forced to wear particular clothes.

Among female homosexuals themselves, discussion of the various possibilities open to us is still limited to small groups who have not appeared in public, or else it is not considered an important issue. The desire for self-identification remains a private matter. These possibilities include butch/femme role-playing as a form of exploiting government gender ideology.[17] Thus, on the one hand, the butches are concerned with legalizing lesbian organizations, while the femmes are interested in forming their own version of Dharma Wanita, something that arouses mixed feelings in women's NGOs.[18] The issues and problems facing female homosexuals in Indonesia are also related to class, educational background and local culture or the town in which they live. This combination of factors forms the structures of interaction and individual sexual formation and self-identification. The forms of butch and femme have links to lesbian subcultures the world over; at the same time they have a distinct local character. Further research on this is clearly required.

Although the growth of homosexual groups in Indonesia is the most rapid in Asia,[19] people remain in fear of social and political oppression if a group is registered as representing female homosexuals. Although homosexuality is not actually illegal, and there is no official proof of social and political pressure, no male or female homosexual group has yet to be officially registered. Existing male and female homosexual networks may be formally organized, but officially they remain informal groups. The first all-Indonesian lesbian and gay congress was organized secretly and took place in December 1993 without seeking the permission of the local government.

The role and influence of the mass media

Returning to the two news clippings at the beginning of this chapter, I am becoming increasingly aware of just how difficult it is to address certain subjects in Indonesia, at the same time recognizing that people in positions of power are free to make statements on topics of which they have no knowledge. The values espoused by people considered important or powerful are constantly given precedence in Indonesia's paternalistic society. At the time of writing, seminars and workshops are being held more and more frequently to discuss current issues related to feminist ideas; the more this happens, the more powerful leaders and 'experts' make statements in the media emphasizing that feminist thought is not part of Indonesian culture. Meanwhile, the government retains a strong censorship role.

Writing this article has made me look again at the underlying reasons for the opposition to feminism. Despite the backlash effect described by Susan Faludi[20] a few years ago, this and other forms of opposition have been unable to prevent a global shift in the position of women. It is this change in the status quo that has caused the challenge to feminism. In this context, the views expressed in the news clippings at the beginning of this article represent a defence mechanism by the establishment.

Unfortunately since Indonesia is traditionally an oral society, books are not an important source of information.[21] The print media is the primary source of reading material for the general public, and the formative agent for public opinion about female homosexuality. It is also the primary reading for female homosexuals of the middle and lower classes, while those of higher status, who are able to read foreign languages, have access to reading materials and magazines from overseas, and often have opportunities to study in other countries. Receiving the news in a form which further constructs and reinforces the subordination of women, the public rarely forms any alternative opinion about the position of women, let alone their sexuality. Feminist thought has started to be the subject of discussion, but only within the confines of workshops and seminars, the influence of which is extremely limited compared with that of the print and electronic media. The mass media conveys the bias of its journalists,[22] and once public opinion has been formed it is difficult to change.

The mass media claims stridently that homosexuality is not Pan-casilaist, and people making such claims are accorded high status in Indonesia's paternalistic society. At the 1994 United Nations International Conference on Population and Development in Cairo, no less than the President and various ministers spoke against homosexuality. The public is socialized to believe what their leaders say, and such condemnation increases social sanctions and the oppression of homosexuality.[23] This is similar to the accusation that feminism exerts a Western influence on Indonesian culture. My own monitoring of the media has pinpointed two periods when the issue of female homosexuality was covered in various places.[24] The first period occurred in 1982–83, when the media presented the issue of female homosexuality as a social phenomenon. This began with the reporting of a female same-sex marriage in the magazine *Tempo* (23 May 1981).[25] The second period covers the years 1987–89, when reports tended to give the impression that homosexuality is caused by Western influence, and is a sexual deviancy which must be cured. Both periods were characterized by stereotyping and moral justification.[26]

The discourse on Indonesian feminism clearly needs to begin from a basic understanding of the situation of Indonesian women, although this does not mean that the idea of feminism should be rejected out of hand because of its source in Europe. Many countries throughout the world have succeeded in locating women's problems in local social conditions, but this process has been limited in Indonesia because of the government's own defence mechanism and its desire to control the role of women. In connection with this, the discourse about sexuality has also been slow to develop. Oppression and control of sexuality has allowed no space for anything other than heterosexuality, with the result that even the Indonesian women's movement has not given a place to female homo-sexuals or other sexual minorities. This space has necessarily been created by female homosexuals themselves.

The mass media is the primary source of information, and still uses this role to convey stereotyped and false information about homosexuality. Because of the government's continuing heavy-handed censorship, issues considered to be out of line with government policy are rarely addressed: for instance, the issue of sexuality is still considered subversive and not in accordance with government programmes for family-planning and creat-ing the ideal family unit. This continued suppression has not prevented female homosexuals from creating the space for their own subculture, but it explains why this subculture remains so hidden.

ACKNOWLEDGEMENT

I would like to acknowledge the assistance of my lesbian friends in the preparation of this article, Dr Monika Reinfelder for giving me this opportunity and for her patience in awaiting it, as well as Dr Alison Murray for her translation and constructive advice.

NOTES

1. B.J.D. Gayatri 'Coming out but remaining hidden: a portrait of lesbians in Java' Thirteenth International Congress on Anthropological and Ethnological Sciences in Mexico City, July 1993, conference paper to be published. Gayatri 'Coming out but remaining oppressed: lesbians in Indonesia, a report for human rights', unpublished.
2. Julia I. Surakusuma 'The state and sexuality in Indonesian New Order', International Conference on the Construction of Gender and Sexuality in East and Southeast Asia, 9–11 December, Los Angeles, unpublished conference paper.
3. Indonesia's New Order government was formed after a bloody coup in 1965, the previous government is known as the Old Order.
4. Saskia Wieringa Uw Toegenegen Dora D. (Amsterdam: Uitgeverij Furie. 1987).
5. Wardah Hafidz 'Gerakan Perempuan Dulu, Sekarang, dan Sumbangannya kepada Transformast Bangsa', Kompas, 21 April 1992 pp.4–5.
6. Dharma Wanita is an organization that was set up to enable the wives of civil servants to support their husbands in their careers. See Saskia Wieringa 'The perfume nightmare: some notes on the Indonesian women's movement' (The Hague: Institute of Social Studies, 1985, working paper). See also Suryakusuma, 'The state and sexuality'.
7. Gayatri, 'Coming out but remaining hidden'.
8. Ibid.
9. J. Patrick Gray, 'Growing yams and men: an interpretation of Kimaam male ritualised homosexual behaviour', in Evelyn Blackwood (ed.), Many Faces of Homosexuality: Anthropological Approaches to Homosexual Behaviour (New York: Harrington Park Press, 1986). Dede Oetomo 'Homoseksualitas di Indonesia', Prisma vol. 7 (July 1991), pp.15–23. Gayatri, 'Coming out but remaining hidden'.
10. For an explanation of why female homosexuals have preferred to remain hidden, see Gayatri, 'Coming out but remaining hidden', and Alison Murray 'Where are the Indonesian lesbians?', Inside Indonesia (March 1995), pp. 22–23.

11. The term 'lesbian' is used outside of the female homosexual community.
12. Murray, 'Indonesian lesbians', and Suryakusuma, 'The state and sexuality'.
13. Alison J. Murray, *No Money No Honey: A Study of Street Traders and Prostitutes in Jakarta* (Singapore: Oxford University Press, 1991).
14. Susie Bright, *Susie Sexpert's Lesbian Sex World* (Pittsburgh: Cleis Press, 1990).
15. ALN (Asian Lesbian Network) is a lesbian network inside and outside Asia. In countries with many lesbian groups, such as Japan, umbrella groups are formed at the national level such as ALN-Nippon. ALN-Taiwan uses this label, as there is no other lesbian organization. Two problems arise for me: the desire to support this network, and the fact that there are a number of female homosexual groups in Indonesia. Since becoming active in ALN I have used the title ALN-Indonesia both for functional purposes and to obscure the existence of other networks, as my friends have requested.
16. I use the term 'lesbian' here as this is the word commonly used by female homosexuals elsewhere in Asia.
17. Wieringa, *Dora D.*
18. Murray, *No Money No Honey*; Suryakusuma, 'The state and sexuality'; Wieringa, 'The perfume nightmare'. This is also based on discussions with Wieringa regarding her contacts with female homosexuals in Indonesia in 1981–82.
19. Murray, 'Indonesian lesbians'.
20. Susan Faludi, *Backlash: The Undeclared War Against Women* (London: Vintage, 1992).
21. As a point of information, based on an interview with an Indonesian publisher, most print runs for books total 3,000–5,000 copies, which usually sell out in 2–5 years depending on the book: for instance, economics titles sell faster than social sciences or philosophy. These numbers are tiny in comparison to Indonesia's population.
22. Debra H. Yatim, 'Gender dalam media massa', in Fauzie Ridjal *et al.*, *Dinamika Gerakan Perempuan de Indonesia* (Yogyakarta: Tiara Wacana, 1993).
23. Gayatri, 'Coming out but remaining oppressed'.
24. Translation Group, *Gays in Indonesia: Selected Articles from Print Media* (North Carlton: Translation Group, 1984). See also Gayatri, 'Coming out but remaining oppressed'.

25. See also Translation Group, *Gays in Indonesia*, and Gayatri, 'Coming out but remaining hidden'.
26. Gayatri, 'Coming out but remaining oppressed'.

lesbian lobby:
apartheid's closet

gertrude fester

As lesbian women living in the large urban centre of Cape Town, we have found it relatively easy to find other lesbians; but lesbians who are for lesbians are thin on the ground indeed. It seems that the misogynist and homophobic values of the heterosexual patriarchy are very firmly entrenched in our own communities.[1]

As a black[2] woman who has been centrally involved in the mass women's movement since 1982, I would agree with the above writers that it was relatively easy to find other lesbians. My assessment of the link between broader women's groups and the organized lesbian movement is based on my experience in the Western Cape, and is largely limited to this area. The existence of a subculture of lesbians was evident – evident, yes, but only if you were aware of it. There were various women who were always together, and who raised certain issues, and your deduction that they were lesbians was in most cases correct. Some lesbians had a social and supportive circle outside of their political work. According to this writer's experience there never was a consensus among lesbians on when or where to raise lesbian issues. However, because of the invisibility and the lack of awareness around lesbian issues in the early 1980s in the mass women's movement, the majority of women were unaware of them.

Another reason why lesbian issues in the women's movement were not even marginal is because the women's movement in South Africa is very complex, a situation I tried to explore at the First Women's Conference in Africa and the African Diaspora.[3] Yes, apartheid was such a fundamental issue that every other concern had to, and definitely did take second place; or, in fact, was relegated to non-issue status. A conspicuous example was the virtually unopposed building of the Koeberg nuclear power-station, hardly 30km from the metropolis of Cape Town.

Yes, I too agree that there were very few lesbians organizing actively for lesbian rights, but the reasons for this are equally complex. Black women in women's organizations never linked their activities in lesbian organizations and women's liberation organizations. This may be explained partly by the alienation they themselves had experienced in mainly white lesbian organizations. But the main reason, I believe, is because it would have alienated them from the majority of black women, they did not have the courage to come out, and the 'central struggle' against apartheid was too overwhelming.

In 1983 LILACS (Lesbians in Love and Compromising Situations) was small and elite and mostly white. It is interesting to note that in their description of lesbian movements, Armour and Lapinsky never alluded to the central issue of racism within the organized lesbian movement. Maybe it did not occur to them, but black women within LILACS never felt comfortable. Open racist statements were often made. The question I would like to ask is: to what extent did black women identify with a small group of white women on the basis of sexual orientation? In LILACS, political concerns such as national liberation were never an issue. At the first Women's Conference in Africa and the African Diaspora I raised the question of solidarity of women across race and class and the seeming impossibility of sisterhood. Even today in 1995 the Women's National Coalition[4] is struggling to develop some sort of united women's voice.

A debate that confronted the broader women's movement in the early 1980s was whether women's liberation was contradictory or supplementary to national liberation. Other questions included to which issues should women activists devote their main energies, and how do you promote both causes (women's liberation and national liberation), if in fact they are two causes? There have been criticisms in the past that by organizing separately, women have 'divided the struggle'. I would argue that they are not separate causes; rather they complement each other. Yet there were times when women had to be strategic about what they were going to emphasize or prioritize. Therefore, women organized separately in, for example, the United Women's Organization (UWO),[5] but still worked towards both women's and national liberation.

A similar dilemma faced black lesbian activists: what do you emphasize – lesbian issues or women's liberation and national liberation? The majority of black lesbians, given the contradictions of their lives in which they faced racism by white lesbians and anti-lesbianism by oppressed black people, identified with the struggle for national and women's liberation in general. Women classified as African by the apartheid regime were subjected to severe oppression and repression. Their movements restricted by influx control,[6] they could not live in an urban area unless they had a pass. The issuing of the pass was subject to a job and a place to stay. Women coming from rural areas had no access to formal housing and therefore had to build their own houses. Those living in informal housing were threatened daily by the police. There was usually no access to water in areas of informal housing, or if there was, one tap had to be shared by hundreds of people. Women engaged in anti-apartheid activities were on the run from the police, a situation that worsened during the state of emergency;[7] when many became political detainees.[8]

These are just some of the issues that affected black women in apartheid South Africa. And yes, few black women activists were part of predominantly white lesbian organizations. But in the face of such repressions black lesbian activists took a political stand to work for national and women's liberation. As part of this struggle lesbianism and other issues were indirectly taken up but definitely not prioritized. Ideally, and in retrospect I see that these issues could have been more integrated. It would have been some way of politicizing people, introducing them to environmental issues, developing an awareness about people who are differently abled and about sexual politics. However, these issues have developed organically and are an integral part of mainstream politics in 1995. But speakers are still cautious and strategic as to when and where they raise issues around sexual politcs.

As stated earlier, LILACS was the first lesbian-only organization in Cape Town. According to Armour and Lapinsky this was inspired and encouraged by the emergence of the Gay and Lesbian Association (GALA) on the University of Cape Town's campus. Meetings took place on Friday nights at the then Glendower Hotel in Rosebank, Cape Town. At the height of apartheid this was in a whites-only suburb, where all amenities were racially exclusive. It is important to contextualize LILACS, as it needs to be highlighted to what extent it was not accessible to black lesbians. It must be noted that there was never any intention to broaden out and become more inclusive. It was a small elite group of white, dominantly English-speaking, middle class, university students and professionals that included a sprinkling of Afrikaans-speaking working-class women. In fact, I remember exactly one Afrikaans-speaking working-class woman, and I do not recall more than three black women ever attending at any one time.

The programme was varied, although it was primarily a social one. There was a special room adjoining the bar. So, armed with mostly beers and a few hard spirits the programme would begin. Ranging from the screening of films to discussions, the topics included women and space, presented by an architect; the persecution of women/'witches' during the Middle Ages; and discussions around the balance of activities, for example whether LILACS should be solely social or include some feminist discussions. At one stage it was suggested that the group should compare the oppression of lesbians to the oppression of black people in the country, but the majority seemed not to be interested in such discussion. Attempts by black women, with the support of a few white progressive women, resulted in the screening of *Jamielah*, a film highlighting the participation of Jamielah and other women in the Algerian liberation struggle against French colonialism. The group also produced a monthly newsletter, which was compiled by a rotating editorial committee. This was distributed widely, including to non-members. Lesbians (especially those in the closet) found the existence of this newsletter very comforting.

In 1983 political activism against apartheid increased, with the formation of the United Democratic Front (UDF) in August. This was an umbrella organization for anti-apartheid groups that focused its attention on mobilizing against the 'racist election' for the Tri-Cameral government.[9] The involvement of black lesbian activists in the UDF and the racism experienced in LILACS caused many of these activists to leave LILACS. Armour and Lapinsky claim that from 1984 onwards attendance at LILACS dwindled and by the end of 1985 the group had ceased to exist. It is the author's contention that at no stage did LILACS, as an organization, want to link with the broader women's movement, nor did the few women involved in progressive politics merge their two interests.

In June 1986 a small number of Cape Town activists organized themselves as Lesbians and Gays Against Oppression (LAGO). This is the first time in the history of South Africa that there was an attempt to link the issue of lesbian and gay rights to broader political rights. In 1987 LAGO became OLGA (Organization of Lesbian and Gay Activists), with the aim of working towards 'a non-racial South Africa free of all forms of oppression, focusing in particular on the oppression of lesbians and gay men'.[10] Just as black lesbian activists never prioritized lesbian issues in the mass political organizations, white lesbians never raised it either. OLGA never attempted to establish a working relationship with the mass-based women's organizations. An overture was made, however, by the Congress of Pink Democrats[11] to the United Women's Congress (UWCO)[12] informing UWCO of their existence and their aims. And OLGA applied to become an affiliate to the UDF. To a certain extent this resulted in some discussions around lesbian and gay issues in mass-based organizations. It has to be noted that once OLGA had been admitted as an affiliate its delegates to general council were also very vociferous, asserting their presence and therefore the issue.

In August 1987 the Federation of South African Women (FEDSAW) was relaunched.[13] Its activities included, among others, organizing the First Women's Cultural Festival, to be held over the weekend of 16–17 April 1988.[14] It was at this juncture that a concrete link was formed between the broad women's movement and lesbians. Part of the two-day festival would be devoted to a morning fête, where various organizations had stalls – for either information and/or fundraising. Invitations went out to various organizations inviting them to have a stall. Each organization would then pay FEDSAW R50 for the hire of the space, and affiliates would donate some percentage of profits to FEDSAW. We also encouraged the stall-holders to inform any other groups who might be interested in participating. At one of the planning meetings held at Community Arts Project in District Six in November 1987, a request came from OLGA for a stall. Someone then asked what OLGA was. After the acronym was explained the next question was, 'What do you mean by lesbian and gay?' The explanation was followed by stunned silence. I think the lesbian women deliberately waited for direction from other women. After a while one of the township women nonchalantly stated that there was no reason why OLGA should not have a stall.[15] It has to be noted that on this occasion there was no animosity or homophobia expressed by the women of the broader women's formations. It should also be remembered that most of the women were very religious, the majority being Christian, with a few Muslims.

Even though there was no open hostility one should point out that there have been cases where lesbian relationships have not been acknowledged within the progressive movement. In two cases of detention from the late 1980s, one overnight and the second for one year, the partners of the two women, although longstanding, were not given due recognition. In the first case a woman comrade informed the arrested woman's estranged biological family, who live in another city, and not her lover, although she was very much aware of their lesbian relationship. The second case naturally attracted a lot of attention and UWCO held campaigns calling for the release of the women political detainees. It was during this time that many UWCO members heard about the lesbian relationship. Apparently in one branch of UWCO some women felt that the two lesbians ought to be censured. It was only through the political intervention of and explanation by a senior woman comrade that they changed their minds. Although whether it made them question their homophobia is doubtful.

The ANC in exile was also challenged on its record of homophobia. It is quite widely known that Ruth Mompati, a senior National Executive Committee member, made some rather homophobic comments in 1987 which were published in *Capital Gay*. She claimed that homosexuality is foreign to South African blacks: 'I cannot even begin to understand why people want gay rights. The gays have no problems. They have nice houses and plenty to eat. . . . No one is persecuting them.'[16]Apparently there was an international outcry by anti-apartheid activists, many of whom were either lesbian or gay. The ANC leadership in exile had to rectify this position by stating publicly that the ANC is against all forms of oppression, including oppression against people because of their sexuality.

On the 2 February 1990 the ANC, Pan Africanist Congress (PAC) and the South African Communist Party (SACP) were unbanned. The stage was set for negotiations and imminent liberation. OLGA worked vociferously to lobby the ANC. The ANC draft Bill of Rights acknowledged OLGA's contribution in its introduction, stating that it had benefited from 'receiving proposals from a wide range of organizations . . . including those concerned with . . . lesbian and gay rights . . . '. The bill, which included provisions on sexual orientation, was accepted by the ANC's National Policy Conference in May 1992. Article 7(2) reads: 'Discrimination on the grounds of gender, single parenthood, legitimacy of birth or sexual orientation shall be unlawful.'

OLGA continued its lobbying role and made submissions to the Convention for a Democratic South Africa (CODESA)[17] in March 1992. The stage was thus set by intensive and consistent lobbying. It needs to be noted that in its lobbying efforts OLGA never approached the women's organizations to support them and hence strengthen their position. The results of OLGA's lobbying was that the interim constitution of South Africa guarantees the rights of all, stipulating that 'there should be no discrimination based on grounds of . . . sexual orientation' (Chapter 3.8), apparently the only constitution in the world that guarantees this. The challenge today, however, with the rise of fundamentalism, is to retain this clause in the final constitution, which is being formulated at the time of writing.[18]

The trial of Winnie Mandela represented another case of high-profile homophobia. On 4 February, 1991 she and three others were charged with kidnapping and assault with intention to commit grievous bodily harm. The defence used the argument that Winnie Mandela and the others had rescued these children from a home where homosexual practices were taking place. In the trial, accusations were made against a Methodist priest, Paul Verryn, who had set up the home for street children. According to Mandela and Falati (one of the co-accused), they had rescued the children from sexual abuse. Obviously this trial attracted high-profile media attention with crowds protesting outside the courtroom in support of Winnie Mandela, often sporting placards with homophobic statements.

During this time many ANC members became extremely concerned about the homophobia that the trial was creating, as well as feeling very ambivalent about the accusations against Winnie Mandela. Many branches of the ANC wrote to the National Executive Council (NEC) asking them to issue a statement on the trial. There was no response. At a general council meeting, addressed by an NEC member, Steve Tswete, and held in Athlone at the then ANC Cape Town head offices, the issue of Winnie Mandela was again raised. A member from the Cape Town branch requested that the NEC give some direction on how to deal with the accusations against her. The speaker claimed that it was very difficult to recruit new members for the ANC with all the negative publicity surrounding the case. Tswete assured members that the NEC would look into it. It never did. To date there is still incredible division on this subject.

The pre-election phase gave rise to many new political parties. However, the only party that had lesbian and gay rights as part of its manifesto was the ANC. As a result, the ANC was the target of much ridicule during campaigns, especially from the myriads of religious political parties which arose overnight. It is interesting to note that the two new women's political parties, the Women's Rights Peace Party (contesting nationally) and the South African Women's Party (contesting regionally in the Western Cape), never raised the issue of lesbianism at all.

It was the sight of fairly high-profile ANC activists addressing lesbian and gay organizations that perhaps strengthened the ANC victory nationally. In retrospect one can say that if there had been a closer working relationship between organized lesbians and the mass democratic women's movement, for example the ANC Women's League in the 1990s, there would have been a change in the consciousness of people towards lesbians and gay men. Yes, we do have the rights of lesbians and gay men protected by the interim constitution, but two other tests lie ahead.

Firstly, there still exists widespread homophobia among people at grassroots level. Lesbian issues are acknowledged and respected by some academics, middle-class people and politicians. Many working-class communities such as the 'Cape Coloureds' have always acknowledged the rights of lesbians and gay men, but homophobia seeps through the media, educational institutions and the largely Christian South African society. A certain degree of hypocrisy or contradiction also exists: many South Africans are vocally anti-lesbian and anti-gay, and yet have family members who are lesbian or gay. They pretend not to notice and do not articulate it. Some of the most prominent women in this country are closet lesbians, and the lesbian cause would be greatly advanced if it became public knowledge.

The second test for South Africa's democracy is whether the clause guaranteeing rights for all irrespective of sexual orientation will be maintained in the final constitution. The rise of the organized fundamentalists and their obviously well-financed campaigns against homosexuality and against a pro-choice stance is quite startling.

The Gay Coalition[19] should increase its lobbying, not as at present only at government level but in the context of the broad spectrum of progressive forces. It is only in this way that the progressive lobby, with its meagre financial resources, will be able to counter the onslaught from the right.

NOTES

1. Mary Armour and Sheila Lapinsky 'Lesbians in love and compromising situations: lesbian feminist organizing in the Western Cape', in Mark Gevisser and Edwin Cameron (eds), *Defiant Desire: Gay and Lesbian Lives in South Africa* (Johannesburg: Ravan Press, 1994), pp. 295–96.
2. Within the progressive movement, especially after rise of Black Consciousness in the early 1970s and the 1976 uprisings, the term 'Black' was used for all persons living in South Africa who did not have the franchise. This included persons classified by the previous apartheid regime as 'coloured' (people with mixed heritage, descendants of the first indigenous people of the Cape, the Khoisan), Asians and Africans indigenous to Southern Africa and who speak indigenous languages as their mother tongue. However, it must be noted that these 'various black' people were not homogenous and were subjected to different degrees of oppression. 'Coloured' and Asian people were not as oppressed as the African people. Their movements were not curtailed by passes and influx control. Within the apartheid ideology African people had to be confined to homelands or Black Bantustans. If they

had jobs in the white enclaves of South Africa their passes were endorsed and they could freely move around in white South Africa. When Africans were caught in the urban areas in search of jobs and their passes had not been endorsed, they were arrested. Hundreds of thousands of people had been imprisoned because of 'pass offences'. African women were particularly affected. African males had easier access to jobs (also migrant labour). Many women came to the urban areas to search for their 'lost' husbands or to escape the poverty of rural homelands, only to be arrested. The Western Cape Province was previously declared a 'Coloured Labour Preference Area'. This meant that apart from the usual discrimination experienced by all black people, coloured labour was the preferred or favoured labour in this area.

3. Gertrude Fester, 'Towards a South African women's movement: bridging activism and Academy'. Paper presented at the First Women's Conference in Africa and the African Diaspora, Nsukka, Nigeria, June 1992.

4. The Women's National Coalition was initiated by the ANC Women's League in 1992. It consisted of the entire range of political organizations, cultural and community groups. Its sole mandate was to consult women nationally to collect their demands for effective equality for women in the new South Africa. It is claimed that five million women were consulted and two million women were involved in the process. These demands were published as the Women's Charter. Copies were presented to the premiers of the nine provinces and the state president on 9 August 1994 (South African Women's day). In June 1994 the mandate was extended to include popularizing the charter (translated into the eleven official languages, as well as braille), training women in advocacy and lobbying skills and empowering rural women.

5. The United Women's Organization was the first mass-based organization in the country following the banning of political groups in the 1960s. It was a non-racial organization, which meant that despite the stringent apartheid laws, women from all 'races' worked side by side for national and women's liberation. It was launched in 1981. There have been criticisms in the past that women's organizations like UWO never considered women's liberation an issue. All UWO literature and speeches made reference to the triple oppression of women: oppressed as black people, as workers and as women, and for the true

liberation of South Africans women had to be freed from these oppressions.

6. A highly complex and expensive system had been developed to monitor and control the movements of 'African' people. Forced to become citizens of an ethnic homeland, even though they had never been there in their lives, mass removals and 'endorsing' out of areas designated as 'white' areas were a frequent occurrence.

7. From 1983 mass protests erupted throughout South Africa against the Nationalist government's new dispensation of 'Tri-Cameral government'. This implied that there would be separate 'houses' in Parliament for Indians (House of Delegates), Coloureds (House of Representatives) and whites (House of Assembly). However, the houses of Delegates and Representatives together included fewer members than the House of Assembly. Hence people protested against this 'puppet' government and the fact that the majority of South Africans were left out. The government then proclaimed a state of emergency, giving police draconian powers.

8. Even though many women have been detained during this period, very little world attention was focused on them. They were scattered in various prisons, and fought their battles in isolation, especially in the rural areas. Women had no Robben Island, which later became known as the political university.

9. Opposition to the Tri-Cameral government mobilized previously alienated groups. It brought together Jews for Justice, The Call of Islam, various Christian denominations, trade unions and small traders like the Western Cape Traders' Association.

10. Derrick Fine and Julia Nicol, 'The lavender lobby: working for lesbian and gay rights within the liberation movement', in Gevisser and Cameron, *Defiant Desire*, p. 270.

11. The Congress of Pink Democrats existed in the late 1980s and functioned as a national umbrella organization for progressive lesbian and gay groups. It is important to note that the choice of the word 'Congress' meant aligning itself to the congress movement – supporting the then banned ANC.

12. UWCO was formed in March 1986 when the United Women's Organization and the Women's Front amalgamated. In June 1990 UWCO dissolved to form the ANC Women's League.

13. The Federation of South African Women was formed in April 1954. It consisted of the ANC Women's League, women from the Congress of Democrats and the Coloured People's Congress and some trade

unions, e.g. the Food and Canning Workers' Union. It was never banned, but in the early 1960s its leadership were either imprisoned, banned, forced underground or in exile. In August 1987 the Western Cape relaunched FEDSAW.

14. In order to promote unity among women, festivals were held over two days, and consisted of cultural activities celebrating women's creativity.

15. People indigenous to Africa and who speak an indigenous African language like Xhosa, Zulu, Pedi, etc. were classified by the previous apartheid regime as African. Because they lived in township (sub-economic) areas they were and still are today in post-apartheid South Africa referred to as Township People. Organizations that supported the ANC believed in African working-class leadership, hence very controversial issues like allowing OLGA to have a stall would usually have to wait for direction from the townships. Some believe that this broad acceptance of developing and supporting only African working-class leadership has contributed to renewed racism and tension in Cape Town between people previously classified as coloured and African.

16. Mark Gevisser 'A different fight for freedon: a history of South African lesbian and gay organization from the 1950s to 1990s', in Gevisser and Cameron, *Defiant Desire*, p. 70.

17. Convention for a Democratic South Africa preceded the multi-party talks which eventually led to the negotiated settlement, the interim constitution and the April 1994 elections.

18. An attempt was made to broadly consult South Africans in the writing of the new constitution. Advertisements in all media encouraged people to make submissions outlining what they thought should be included. The constitution will then be formulated according to these submissions. This process will culminate in the final constitution, which is supposed to be completed by May 1996. According to sources working with the submissions, many have come from organized fundamentalists protesting against the inclusion of rights for lesbians and gay men.

19. The Gay Coalition consists of all the lesbians and gay groups nationally who campaign for lesbian and gay rights in South Africa.

7

liz frank and elizabeth khaxas

What they did to us
telling us that black was not so beautiful
we should be slightly lighter
Use He-Man, Ambi . . .
then we will look so beautiful

What they did to us
telling us crizzy coarse hair was not so beautiful
our hair should be slightly straighter
Use skinstraight, soft-a-silky . . .
then all the men would love us dearly

What they did to us
telling us roundness was not so beautiful
we should be slightly slender
Use slimline, kilo-stop . . .
then all the men would like to marry us

To them skin lighteners, my sisters
I say voertsak, voertsak
My skin is my own
I don't want a lighter kind of love

To them hair straighteners, my sisters
I say voertsak, voertsak
My hair is my own
I don't want a straighter kind of love

To them diet poisons, my sisters
I say voertsak, voertsak
I don't want a slender kind of love

'Black Sisters' by Elizabeth Khaxas (1994)[1]

Lesbians are still almost invisible in our country. But we do exist! We are a small and diverse community in a small and diverse population. And we are a divided community, divided by the barriers that the long history of colonial oppression and apartheid has left in our people.[2] White and coloured lesbians are a little more visible than black lesbians. The latter may know (of) others in their own cultural group, but apartheid has kept them distant from black lesbians of other cultural groups.

But there is a mood of change in the air. With the achievement of independence in 1990, the human rights and dignity of our people were enshrined in the new constitution and brought to bear on all aspects of our lives. There is a growing sense of the rights and freedoms of the individual in an open and democratic society. Many of us are engaged in the process of building trust and understanding across the barriers of race and ethnic group to find our common interests as lesbians, and to support one another in coming out. Two groups in particular have become publicly active on lesbian issues since 1993. One is the feminist collective SISTER Namibia, of which we are members. The other is the Gay and Lesbian Organization of Namibia (GLON).

The SISTER Collective was formed in 1989, the year in which the first democratic elections were held after more than one hundred years of foreign rule. The main activity of the collective is to produce the feminist magazine *SISTER Namibia*, which aims to speak out against all forms of oppression and discrimination against women, and to write women back into Namibian history. In 1993, the collective added the struggle against homophobia to its publicly stated aims of combating sexism and racism. A small number of articles, short stories, poems and letters dealing with lesbian life and lesbian issues have appeared in the magazine since then, as well as in an anthology of women's writings produced by the collective in 1994.

The GLON was formed two years ago. Its first aim is to become officially registered as a non-governmental organization (NGO) which provides counselling for lesbians and gay men, including HIV/AIDS counselling. Once this has been achieved, various donors are ready to provide the necessary funds. GLON is also a lobbying organization for lesbian and gay rights. Two GLON members made lesbian and gay history in Namibia in

July 1995 when they came out to the nation in a government-sponsored newspaper which is widely read throughout the country.

GLON members also came out in reaction to news reports that there are moves afoot within the evangelical Lutheran Church in Namibia to ban lesbians and gay men from being or becoming pastors. GLON announced that the organization was in the process of setting up a church for lesbians and gay men with the assistance of a similar church in South Africa. Approximately 90 per cent of Namibians are Christians. Missionaries from the UK, Germany and Finland carried the Bible to most corners of our country over the past 150 years, translating it into all the local languages. Many churches played an active and courageous role in the liberation struggle, but their leadership is generally very conservative on issues of social life and morality, quoting from the Bible to support their views. They do not condone the use of the condom for birth control or protection against HIV/AIDS, but preach fidelity within and celibacy outside marriage. They describe homosexuality as immoral, sinful and evil.

By preaching celibacy outside marriage, the Church is totally out of touch with Namibian reality. The high proportion of single mothers with on average five children is strong evidence at least of widespread heterosexual activity outside marriage. In some cultural groups, the pressure on women to have children is stronger than the pressure to get married. Men expect women to prove their fertility before considering marriage, but then often abandon both mother and child. Women have a string of children from different fathers in the hope that the father of their next child will marry them and help to provide for the family.

Teenage pregnancies are common, and are an indication of the social pressures on girls to have sexual relations with their boyfriends without adequate knowledge of contraceptive protection. Poverty is one of the reasons why schoolgirls become involved with sugar daddies, often their own teachers! Sex education was taboo before independence, and now the main focus is on the prevention of HIV/AIDS, which according to the latest figures is spreading rapidly, particularly among schoolgirls and young women. Male homosexuality is mentioned in HIV/AIDS education, but lesbianism is still a taboo topic.

The social pressure on women to have boyfriends and to prove their womanhood through bearing children may be one reason why lesbianism has been such a taboo subject. There are also severe economic pressures on women to conform to society's expectations of their role. More than 30 per cent of our people are unemployed, many more underemployed. The number of women working in professions in the public sector, banks and businesses is small compared to the vast majority of women who work as farmers or domestic workers, or are unemployed. Being financially dependent on one's family or boyfriend does not leave much room for establishing an individual lifestyle as a lesbian.

Gender stereotypes are strong in our society. In the urban areas in particular, women spend time and money emulating the fashion models in the glossy magazines, which dictate beauty standards imported from the West. Black women use chemicals to straighten their hair and bleach their skin, the latter eventually burning dark scars into their faces.

White rule and apartheid have also left deep scars in the psyche of our people, and in particular of black women, who were despised by whites both for their blackness and their womanhood. Standing up proudly for one's identity as a black Namibian woman takes courage. How much more courage does it take to break the culture of silence and stand up proudly as a black lesbian!

Developing a sense of lesbian identity and pride has been easier for white and coloured women in Namibia. Women of European origin have had opportunities to make contact with lesbian communities in their 'mother countries'. White and coloured women from South Africa have been able to keep in touch with the lesbian circles in the urban centres there. Black Namibian women who have had the chance to attend women's conferences in Cape Town and Johannesburg or the international feminist book fairs in Amsterdam and Melbourne, have described it as a liberating shock to suddenly find themselves surrounded by open lesbians.

The process of coming together and coming out as lesbians in Namibia has begun at last. We look across our southern border in admiration of the long history of lesbian and gay lobbying that as been part of the anti-apartheid struggle in South Africa. Because the histories of our two countries have been so intertwined, we tend to compare our struggles and try to fathom the differences that have emerged. Why did the struggle for lesbian and gay rights never become part of the agenda of the Namibian liberation movement?

From the early 1960s, the liberation struggle was led by the South West Africa People's Organization (SWAPO). Over the next thirty years, tens of thousands of Namibians left the country to join the movement in exile. They became guerrilla fighters in the liberation army or received training in a broad range of fields through the United Nations and many countries around the world, in preparation for self-rule after independence. In 1966 SWAPO took up the armed struggle against the South African occupation, and northern Namibia became a war zone. All the efforts of SWAPO were focused on mobilizing people for the independence struggle. Young women as well as men underwent military training, and a number of women joined the liberation army.

In 1969 the SWAPO Women's Council was formed to recruit more women to the struggle; and the women in exile organized the daily life of the refugee communities in Angola and Zambia. The SWAPO Women's Council aimed to achieve equality for women through education and political participation. Gender roles were challenged and women experienced empowerment, in particular through their political and military involvement in the struggle. But the struggle for national liberation remained the paramount goal, and women were careful not to antagonize their male comrades with charges of sexism, and stand accused of being divisive. To be elected into leadership positions within the SWAPO Women's Council, women were expected to be married, and be respectable and acceptable to men.[3]

Inside the country, the SWAPO Women's Council was mainly active in recruiting women for the liberation movement. A grassroots feminist organization, Namibian Women's Voice, was treated with suspicion and opposition for organizing women around specific women's issues during the 1980s. We do not yet know of any lesbians who were involved in the liberation movement, either in exile or at home. But we imagine that the pressure to outwardly conform to the politically correct image of womanhood must have been strong indeed. SWAPO members tell us that lesbianism was never discussed within the organization.

The Namibian Women's Voice, founded in 1985, was the first organization in Namibia which focused specifically on women's issues. It supported the liberation struggle but believed that this had to address and incorporate women's everyday battles for survival in the rural areas and the black townships. Creating income-generating schemes and self-help projects, such as soup kitchens and kindergartens became one of the main activities of the Namibian Women's Voice. This was accompanied by educational programmes, such as literacy training and health education. A third important area of work was leadership training, involving consciousness-raising on gender stereotypes and the discrimination of women in society. But again, lesbianism was never an issue. The political and economic empowerment of poor women in rural areas was the main focus of the work.

When the two of us began to come out as a lesbian couple in women's meetings after independence, we were told by leading SWAPO activists and women in power that 'Namibians are not ready for this yet', despite the fact that one of us is a black Namibian! There is a strong prejudice that lesbianism is not African, not part of the black Namibian culture, but brought here through influences from the West. However, the historical records suggest otherwise.

Written Namibian history began with the diaries and reports of foreign missionaries in the early nineteenth century. They provide evidence of the missionaries' moral and at times physical battles against social practices such as polygyny and premarital sex. There are occasional references to other condemnable 'perversities', but these are never spelled out in more detail. We are left to wonder. The only research known to us that relates specifically to homosexuality in Namibia stems from a German author, Kurt Falk, and was published in 1926. Falk spent ten years in 'South West Africa', and reported to have found evidence of male homosexuality in all cultural groups, and lesbianism in most. For example, he states that among the Herero people, both male and female homosexual activity was widespread, although all women and most men were married. Falk voices the typical male disbelief at lesbians' preference for sex with women. He was amazed that it was not old or 'unmanned' women but predominantly young women, with every opportunity for heterosexual sex, who 'insatiably' practised same-sex intercourse.[4]

We do not yet know of further research that could corroborate or expand on the above, but we have been told that it is still a common and culturally condoned practice in the Herero community for young unmarried men to have sexual relations with their male friends. Sadly, we have made no headway in finding out about the women. The black lesbians we know about are mainly Damara women, as one of us grew up in this community. From our own experiences in the Damara community, we can say that lesbianism is not talked about openly but is passively accepted. We know of professional Damara women who are highly respected in their community, while it is widely known that their life partners are women. After initial reactions of shock and rejection combined with pressure on us to 'reform', our own relationship has been well accepted by family and friends. It remains a challenging and extensive project to research lesbianism in the diverse communities of Namibia, past and present.

The legal situation of lesbians and gay men in Namibia is unclear. At the time of writing, many repressive laws inherited from the long period of South African rule have still not been repealed. The Immorality Act of 1957 prohibits 'unlawful carnal intercourse', which is defined as carnal intercourse between persons who are not married. According to the Attorney

General, this law makes any sexual activity between two people of the same sex a criminal offence, although he is of the opinion that homosexuality should be decriminalized. The Indecent or Obscene Photographic Matter Act of 1967 includes in its long list of prohibitions the possession of photographic matter depicting homosexuality and lesbianism, but this Act is no longer enforced in our country.

The inherited South African laws stand in clear contradiction to the Namibian Labour Act of 1992, which explicitly prohibits discrimination on the grounds of sexual orientation. The constitution of 1990, which is hailed as one of the most democratic constitutions in the world, is not so explicit. However, it is equally vague in the section which guarantees freedom of choice of a marriage partner. Article 14 defines marriage as a relationship between two freely consenting adults. This could be interpreted as giving lesbians and gay men the right to marry in Namibia![5]

Neither the constitution nor the inherited South African laws have been challenged by lesbians and gay men. The South African laws are presently under review, and the Women and Law Reform Committee has been given the task of looking at all legal issues relating to gender. But the law reform process is slow due to the backlog of legislation that needs to be changed, a situation that is compounded by a lack of legal drafters and researchers. It is also unclear precisely which legislation is being redrafted and when, which makes lobbying difficult. We observe that the new South African government is much more active in inviting public input into their country's new legislation.

The uncertain legal situation could be seen as one of the reasons why lesbians have kept such a low profile up to now. Most do not even know of the clause protecting us in the Labour Code. Yet the repressive South African laws have not been enforced in Namibia for many years, even during the final period of South African rule. We know of a number of couples who moved from South Africa to Namibia during the 1980s to escape the persecution of interracial and lesbian love that exists there. No one we have asked, including the State Attorney, can remember a single case of legal prosecution of lesbians or gay men in this country. Is this because we have kept ourselves so invisible up to now instead of challenging this society into revealing and overcoming its homophobia?

The political situation is at present relatively open. We do not know which way Namibia will develop on the issue of lesbian and gay rights. In Zimbabwe President Mugabe has just called on his fellow citizens to arrest, personally, lesbians and gay men and deliver them to police stations (August 1995). In contrast to this, the political climate in South Africa seems to be more open and inclusive of our particular minority, among others. In Namibia, the SWAPO government has a two-thirds majority in Parliament. The party General Secretary stated recently that lesbians and gay men had no place in the party. In contrast, the Prime Minister assured us on a radio programme last year that the Bill of Rights in the constitution guaranteed freedom from discrimination on the grounds of sexual orientation, even though this was not spelled out.

So we do not know which way Namibia will develop on this issue. But we do know that the time has come to speak out as lesbians in our communities and our country. We have experienced the feelings of self-denial, self-betrayal and guilt for too long. We claim our right to affirm ourselves as women who love and nurture women.

Women in politics no longer tell us that 'Namibians are not ready for this yet'. We now hear that lesbian rights are not a priority; issues such as women's poverty and women's needs in health and education are viewed as more important for political action. We see this as another expression of anti-lesbianism. Standing up for lesbian rights takes no butter off anybody's bread, nor does it mean that the economic, social and political empowerment of women should take second place. We assume that there are lesbians in all communities and social strata of our society, so that we are not only speaking out for ourselves or a privileged few. We see lesbian rights as human rights, which are indivisible.

The SISTER collective and the magazine provide an important space in which we can develop our identity and creativity. Working together with other lesbians and supportive heterosexual women has brought us out of our social isolation and strengthened our sense of community. This has heightened our awareness of the need for political action on lesbian issues. Through the magazine we can share all this with our readers, and contribute towards the building of a new society based on new values. We are striving for the appreciation that difference and diversity enrich us all, and that love and partnership come in all kinds.

NOTES

1. Reprinted with permission from SISTER Namibia Collective (ed.), A *New Initiation Song: Writings by Women in Namibia* (Windhoek: SISTER Namibia Collective, 1994).

2. Namibia was a German colony from 1884 to 1915. After the First World War it became a British mandate, but was administered and exploited by white South Africa until 1989.
3. H. Becker, *Namibian Women's Movement 1980 to 1992: From Anti-Colonial Resistance to Reconstruction* (Frankfurt: Verlag für Interkulturele Kommunikation, 1995).
4. K. Falk, 'Homosexualität bei den Eingeborenen in Südwest-Afrika', *Geschlecht und Gesellschaft* (1926) vol. 13, p. 208.
5. J. Diescho, *The Namibian Constitution in Perspective* (Windhoek: Macmillan, 1994).

sisters of mercy

tina machida

Lesbians have always been there in the history of our culture. In the past, they were tortured by having hot round nuts pressed against their backs (referred to in the Shona language as *Rusosera*), which was meant to cure them so they would be able to accept a man. Some lesbians marry but others remain unmarried their whole lives. Many think lesbians are bewitched because they resist being 'cured' no matter what people do to them.

Long ago, young women used to fulfil their lesbian lives away from the prying eyes of their elders when they went to the meadows to herd cows and goats. But most black families in Zimbabwe do not believe lesbianism exists and they refuse to acknowledge it. People believe that you are either mad or bewitched. Once they find out you are 'like that' they take you to the faith healer (*n'anga*) who covers your body with small cuts and smears you with herbs. They steam you in herbs to get rid of the bad spirits, because they believe if you are a woman you are only good enough for marriage. The belief is that if you refuse to get married then someone has bewitched you, so they cut you with razors and dip you in a flowing river so that the bad spirit can flow with the water (*kupumwa mamhepo*). When they realize that nothing they are doing is helping, they decide that you must be disturbed and take you to a psychiatrist or put you in an institution. If they do not have the money for that, then you are treated as an outcast for the rest of you life. And if you do not have the sense to run away, or enough money to work, you are doomed for life.

In the old days, if your parents found out that you were unwilling to marry they would go and seek advice from faith healers, who would tell them you had a male spirit. They had to comply with the culture and do what had to be done with women like that. These women had to marry other women because they represented a male. The parents would brew beer at a ceremony (*bira*) celebrating that male spirit. They would put you on a reed mat and cover you in a multicoloured striped cloth (black, white, blue and red), give you a wooden plate, knobkerrie and a wooden stool, and then call a faith healer to come and pronounce you a spirit medium (*svikiro*). From then on you were allowed to marry another woman and look for a man so your wife could bear you children. You were allowed as many wives as you could pay *lobola* (bride price) for.

But if people did not believe that you had a male spirit then your life was restricted. There would be no opportunities to go off alone with women of your own age; you stayed with the older women. So, young women who were lesbians had to tell lies in order to live the way they wanted.

I know about ten lesbians in Zimbabwe who are out to their families. They have all been thrown out of their family homes and have ended up with nowhere to go. Sleeping on the streets and exchanging sex for money are the only means of survival for them. Two committed suicide; they could not bear the misery any longer.

In the early 1980s, we used to meet in Harare in a town park, where we would sit and talk for hours sharing our sorrows and pleasures. Our biggest problem was that we did not have the freedom to meet our lovers privately; so we decided to put our money together at the end of every week to save up for the monthly rent on a room in Epworth (the cheapest place to live in Harare), where the five of us stayed for about three months. We were paying 30 Zimbabwe dollars (about US$4) for the room, and we were able to save a little to put towards food, cooking utensils and clothes.

We tried to do something with our lives to earn money without having to sell our bodies, and to this end we teamed up with black gay men in the Epworth area, and put aside an extra dollar at the end of every week so that we could buy cigarettes, sweets, biscuits and meat. The women would cook pieces of chicken, pancakes and roasted ground nuts and *mazondo* (a sort of stew), and the men would sell what we made in the beer halls. From the profit we made we had enough to pay the rent and food, but there was virtually nothing left over for clothes.

Other teenagers who had also been thrown out of their homes got to hear about our establishment (known as 'the shelter for the wierdos'). In 1991, we gave it the official title of *Ngoni Chaidzo* (Sisters of Mercy). Even today, abandoned people come to us for shelter, but we are crowded and very often have to turn them away if they are under the age of majority, which is twenty-one in Zimbabwe. But if we see they are desperate to the point of suicide, we accept them, on condition that they work as hard as the rest of us. Those we cannot accept we are forced to take to the social welfare office, although we know that the authorities will say they have to go back to their families because they are under age. And when these young people are taken back home they find life there is still unbearable, so they run away again and end up on the streets. We are scared to take them back with us because the police would simply arrest us, saying that we were teaching them bad things.

People come and go, but on average there are usually between six and ten of us to a room. We rent ten rooms altogether and, because we have no privacy and are crowded together, we are always hoping that we will find a donor to come and rescue us from our problem of shelter. We have tried to rent more rooms, but we sometimes get arrested for selling our produce in the beer halls without a hawker's licence, so whatever we might have raised from sales goes to paying the fine and we end up back where we started. This means there is never enough money for what we need, and we are forced to go back to the streets as prostitutes. We all feel insecure, which leads us to quarrel, and many think the best way out is to kill themselves. We have tried to attend counselling courses, but it is expensive for us to go to town and so it is difficult for us to get much information on suicide.

We used to be beaten up by the police once they knew we were lesbians. We are targets for men who think they need to prove that they are better than us. These men think that we are trying to show them that men are not good enough for us, and as a punishment they rape and beat us up and leave us for dead. The police treat it as robbery, unless told to do otherwise – even the police do not want to acknowledge the existence of lesbians.

We are scared to leave our rooms unattended for fear that spiteful people who hate what we represent will steal or burn our property. When we want to go out to a nightclub we travel in a group for fear of being mugged. When we are attacked the police say we invited it to happen. But these days things are changing with the police: they only arrest us if we do something indecent in public, and they no longer arrest us just because they know we are lesbian. Besides, they do not have any chapters about lesbianism in their law books.

There are so many black lesbians in Zimbabwe, but most are afraid to come out because they would immediately lose their jobs. Even those who are known to be lesbian, and who still manage to hold on to their jobs, are shunned and abused by the public, and there is nowhere they can report this abuse.

Most lesbians stay with their parents, because in our culture you are still under the guardianship of your parents if you are not married. These women are scared to come out and go through what some of us did. Mostly, they are scared about security. If you are thrown out of the house, there is no one to look after you – it is dog eats dog. If you are not strong enough to look after and defend yourself, you end up in the gutter – dead!

We often meet closet lesbians and they tell us about their feelings and problems. We cannot invite them to join us, as we do not have enough to look after ourselves never mind the needs of others. The life we lead would seem worse for them, because they have not experienced the hardness of it before and they would find it difficult to survive the crowding of so many into one room.

The parents of these closeted lesbians think their daughters are bewitched because they do not have boyfriends, and the daughters let them think this. They feel guilty because their parents are wasting money taking them to faith healers. Some end up telling the truth, but the parents often ignore them or refuse to believe what they are saying and instead carry on wasting their money. In this modern world parents think that all girls who say they are lesbian are pretending that they have a male spirit because they do not want to get married, and would prefer to become prostitutes. These parents then force men on you.

There is one lesbian we know of who faked possession by a male spirit to escape the problem of men being forced on her by her relatives. She told her parents she was having a recurring dream in which she was a man with many wives at a big place with many huts and children, and that she was wearing animal skins like those our ancestors wore. She secretly went to a faith healer and bribed him to tell her parents that she had a male spirit. Later, her parents went to the faith healer to find out why she was having such dreams and what they meant for their daughter. They were told by the *n'anga* that their daughter had a male spirit and that they were to brew beer so that she could be pronounced and celebrated. The parents did everything they were told, and in the end their daughter was allowed to marry a woman. She paid *lobola* according to the custom and got married.

The couple lived together happily except for the fact that there were no children. Normally, in our custom, when a woman does not bear children, the blood brother of the husband inseminates the woman. In this case, however, the brother knew the truth about his sister and her wife and so refused to have sex with his sister's wife. The parents decided to find another wife who would bear children for their daughter, and this time gave the brother the task of looking for her. He found someone, and the daughter married a woman her brother liked and he slept with her happily. Today, this woman has three wives and four children and is happy with the way her life has turned out. She has no problems with social attitudes; people know the culture and what she stands for.

Some girls run away from home to join the Catholic sisterhood, because they do not want to marry men and would rather stay together as women. In these convents the girls are paired off according to who they like. What goes on behind closed doors nobody knows, but we believe there is much lesbianism practised. The lifestyle is hidden behind the religion, but if you watch you can see the lesbianism and there is no reason to doubt that it will always be there.

My name is Chipo Machida but most people call me Tina, which is a name I was given by my parents immediately after I was born. Most Zimbabwean families give a child this first name as soon as she is born, in order to have something to call their daughter before they decide on a proper name. They call this name in Shona *zita redumba*, which means the first name you have on earth as an inheritance. My family call me by this name, so everyone uses it and I am now more used to it than my proper name.

I am twenty-five years old. I was born in Gokwe, a town 500km south of the capital city, Harare, where I now stay. I completed the first three years of my schooling (grades one to three) in Gokwe before moving to Harare to finish my primary and secondary education. It was when I came to Harare that I found out that I was not like other little girls my age, because I did not want to play with dolls and houses. All I wanted was to play soccer with boys and wear trousers, climb trees and do what the boys were doing. I grew up a tomboy and I never had girlfriends. Girls did not like me anyway because I was bossy and did not want to play house with them.

When I was in form one I had a teacher who liked me so much she would bring me sweets and invite me to her house. I knew I was attracted to her, because I used to look forward to these visits very much. I was very scared of my feelings and frightened that the other students would notice. I did not know what these feelings meant, so I ended up avoiding her.

When I was in form four I got involved with a girl who was doing her A levels. She was nice to me and taught me a lot about myself. She used to take me out to meet some of her friends who were like ourselves, but our relationship did not go any further – she is white and the racial conflict within her community put an end to our good relationship before it could blossom.

I am now with a beautiful black woman and we stay together. We were always on the run because my parents are against what I am. When they discovered I was a lesbian, they tried to force me to find a boyfriend, but I could not fit in with what they wanted. I was afraid that I was going to end up in trouble because of my attitude, so I used to bring a gay man home and tell my parents we were lovers and that we were saving so we could get married. They believed me and he came to dinner with my family once a week. When they found out that we were lying, our weekly dinners were banned and he was not allowed to come back to our house.

My parents decided to look for a husband on my behalf. They brought several men home to meet me but I was not interested, so in the end they forced an old man on me. They locked me in a room and brought him every day to rape me so I would fall pregnant and be forced to marry him. They did this to me until I became pregnant, after which they told me I was free to do whatever I wanted but that I must go and stay with this man or else they would throw me out of the house. They did throw me out eventually, assuming that as I was unemployed, I would end up going to this man's house anyway. Instead, I went to stay with my friends.

I went for an abortion and stayed in hospital for a month. After that I used to hide whenever I saw my relatives. I did not contact them for six months. The police were looking for me, so I used to move during the night only. In the end, the police found me and took me home, where I was locked up and beaten until I could not even lift my arms or get up.

I stayed in that room for months pretending I was very sick so they would not bring the horrible man again, but they did and I fell pregnant again. I ran away and went to stay with my girlfriend. I did not go for an abortion this time, because I was scared it would kill me. The first time had been really painful. I kept the pregnancy until I had a miscarriage at seven months and the baby died. Then I was always on the run. As soon as I knew that my parents had found out where I was staying I moved on to another place. I was scared that this time they would put chains on me, so I was in hiding. I have not seen my family for some time and they are not bothering me anymore, but they have disowned me. They do not want to talk to me.

Black Zimbabweans think that black girls are playing at being lesbian and that they have been brainwashed by whites. They think that being a lesbian is a white man's [sic] disease. When people see a black woman in the company of a white woman they automatically assume they are lesbians, and they shout snide remarks so that the couple feel uncomfortable and unsafe.

I interviewed some lesbian couples and found out that many of the problems were similar. My first interview was with Rose and Tendai, who both seemed very insecure. Rose is white and Tendai is black. They met about a year ago but are living separately, scared to move in together because of the racism within the community. Rose's parents and friends accept her for what she is, but they do not accept her lover because she is black. They say it would be more dignified if she were to have a white lover and that it is socially embarrassing for her to be seen with someone black. They say they are forced to invite a lot of people to each social occasion so that Rose and Tendai's relationship will not be discovered. They have to sneak around, and when they want to be in each other's company privately, they either have to book a hotel room for a night or go to some of Tendai's friends who are sympathetic. Sometimes it is difficult for them to be alone together, and often they go for a month or more just meeting in crowded places. They are frustrated and end up blaming each other instead of finding a solution.

As Rose is still living with her parents and going to college there is no money for them to rent a flat where they would be among people of all colours and away from racism. Rose said that her parents had threatened to cut her out of their will if she kept on with her black lover, so she told them that she had broken off the relationship. Nowadays, when there is a party at her parents' house or that of friends or relatives, Tendai is not invited because it would be immediately obvious that the two were still together. Rose has to go to all functions by herself except those run by GALZ (Gays and Lesbians of Zimbabwe), where nobody cares what you do or with whom as long as you keep your business out of the lives of other people.

As far as Rose is concerned everything would be all right if it was not for the racism of her people. She said they were tense about her lesbianism until they realized she was not the only one, and they accepted that at least she was happy when in lesbian company. Now they do not mind at all what she is. Rose invites them to GALZ parties and the gay games which GALZ organizes and her parents are supportive. Rose told me that at the college she attends the teachers know that she is lesbian and some of them treat her in an offhand manner. They think if you are lesbian then you are stupid and unlikely to be able to pass exams, but Rose shows them that she is as normal and as bright as any straight student. She finds messages in her desk or in her locker ridiculing her, but she does not care what they think of her as long as they do not harm her or her school work. Other than that, she feels she gets what she wants from life.

On the other hand, Tendai is the one constantly in trouble. She was thrown out of the house when her parents found out, and they have disowned her as an African child. There are times when she needs the help of her relatives but she is turned away. She says that she has a problem with her ancestors coming to her in her dreams and telling her that she must go and brew beer in the presence of her relatives so that all her problems can be solved. She has been to so many faith healers and they have all told her the same thing. There is no other way, because she is always in trouble and being arrested for no reason. She has been told that all this would end if she were to brew the beer.

Tendai's parents and relatives have refused to help her, and she says she is going to kill herself because she has no one to turn to. The only place she finds peace and happiness is at a GALZ party or when she meets up with some black lesbians. Her lover is another refuge, but she does not feel free when they are together because she is scared that if Rose's friends and relatives should see them Rose would end up in the same boat as her. She has tried joining those tennis and other clubs which she can afford, but as soon as they know she is a lesbian they find excuses to dismiss her.

Tendai works for a big company in town as an executive secretary. Her employers know she is a lesbian, but they are white and understand this issue better and do not give her any problems. One major difficulty in her workplace is that some of her workmates treat her as if she had a mental health problem, which she resents. She tries everything she can to make them better informed, but this only makes it worse because the women avoid talking to her, saying that maybe she will try it on with them. The men are resentful and accuse her of thinking that she is better than men because she earns more than most of them. They are always trying to put her down. One woman in particular was jealous of Tendai's status at work. This woman went to the point of stealing from the company and then telling the employer that it was Tendai. Luckily, the police found the stolen goods in the woman's home.

Working conditions are bad and Tendai is lonely and always ridiculed. She has been raped three times, though she only reported it the first time because the police said she had invited it by moving around at night with a man. The man who raped her was a workmate who had offered to escort her home. She felt she could not refuse because she needed a friend at work. The man was let off with no charge because he claimed they were lovers and had been sleeping together for some time. These days she does not go out of the house after dark by herself, and her doors and windows have burglar bars and double locks that take five minutes to unlock, both from inside and outside. She is so insecure that you have to be careful what you say to her. She quickly gets angry and is near to crying all the time.

Taona is a woman of twenty, and she reckons her experiences are as bad as those of any other black lesbian in Zimbabwe. Where she grew up it was very difficult for a lesbian; her community in the rural areas was dominated by men. She first knew and understood about herself when she was twelve. She used to play husbands and wives with her girlfriends. They preferred to play together even though there were boys in the community. She always chose to play the role of a man no matter what game they were playing, and playing hide and seek gave her and her girlfriend the chance to kiss and touch. In Taona's words:

> I felt so isolated when the people in the community (in the rural areas where I was living at the time) found out I was different from other girls. Boys were always after me, and when I rejected them they would try to rape me or beat me up. People used to laugh at me because I used to and still work like a man. They would whisper amongst themselves and then laugh.
>
> Things went wrong when my brother caught me naked making love with another girl in my bedroom. He told my parents in front of the village elders during their monthly court [*dare*]. We were beaten up and told that if we did it again they would take us to where the witches [*varoyi*] are brought, a place infested with lions and leopards where we would not have survived for more than five minutes. It put a fear worse than death into us, and we did not do it again.
>
> After that, nobody wanted to talk to or be associated with us for fear that they would end up being beaten by their parents. Life was hell on earth for us at that time. We were expelled from school because the teachers thought we were going to teach other students bad habits. I asked my parents if I could go and learn at another school but they refused, so I became a leper in my own home. As I am the eldest in the family my friends used to consult me on other issues of the family, but from that time onwards they treated my younger sister as the eldest and pretended I did not exist.

Life was unbearable in that village, so Taona decided to run away from home. She stole her mother's money and went to her girlfriend's place to pick her up:

She agreed to come with me, and we slept in the bush that night with no blankets, until morning when we boarded a bus to Harare. When we got to Harare there was nowhere to go, so we slept at the railway station for a week until we were evicted by the police. We then moved to the Mukuvisi river where there were other destitutes staying. We built a shack made of plastic and cardboard boxes. To survive, we picked food from the rubbish bins outside restaurants or stole it from unsuspecting people in restaurants.

When, in the end, she fell sick from eating dirty food and was admitted to hospital for a few weeks, she decided to change her life and stop being a vagrant. She and her girlfriend met up with other street kids who were making a living from shoplifting. She was arrested three times and sentenced to three months in prison with hard labour. Luckily, the magistrate was sympathetic towards street kids and reduced their jail terms. She was sixteen at the time.

One day, after they had been on the streets for a year and two months, she met up with a gay man who took her to Epworth where there were other young women who were lesbians. They were generous and offered everything they had to share.

Taona and her girlfriend are very happy where they are because, although they have their ups and downs, they live like a family. They have started a soap-making project, and are looking for a donor so that they can go into full production and be registered. They enjoy living as a family, and plan what to do to achieve their goals and how to fight oppression.

Interviews with other people showed that each person's situation is different, but also that there are common themes. One woman whose daughter is a lesbian says that she blames no one but herself for the way her daughter has turned out. She said that when she and her husband first got married they agreed to have four boys before they could consider having a girl. When the first-born turned out to be a girl they were very bitter and the father totally ignored his daughter. She grew up trying everything she could think of to be the son they did not have. To make matters worse, after her they had three more girls, which brought great disillusionment into the family and constant quarrelling. There was no happiness in that family.

The daughter did all the things boys do, and only when she finished school and went on a mechanics course and later joined the army did her father start to take an interest in her. She now has a very high rank in the army and her father is very proud of her. He brags that his daughter is better than most men and her achievements are greater than most. This makes it difficult for her to associate with people in her own area. When I talked to her she was very relieved to at last have someone to talk with openly. She told me she has been wearing trousers and boots since as far back as she can remember, and that the only time she has worn dresses was when going to school or the time she went for an interview with the army. She said the way she grew up and the things her father used to say made her want to achieve more than the boys he knew. She said she used to imagine herself as a man and sometimes she would even dress as a man and keep very short hair. She went out at night and took girls on dates, pretending to be what she was not. Sometimes things would go well and she would not be found out but, at times, when discovered, she would simply say that she was a reporter researching for an article. This pretence happened often until she met up with a lesbian, and the two now stay together. Her father pretends he does not see what is happening, but her mother acknowledges it and supports her.

Taona's mother said that she had gone to the faith healers to make sure she would have a baby boy, but things turned out differently. She tried this several times until she gave up. That is when she gave birth to a baby boy – the last born. She said that all the time she used to pray and think that she was going to be blessed with a boy. All her daughters say they feel comfortable in trousers because they are more used to them than dresses, but only one of them has turned out to be lesbian. She believes that maybe if she had not been so hard on her daughter and expected the impossible, Taona might have turned out differently. She has no illusions about Taona getting married to a man or of her having babies.

Some lesbians talk of having had relations with men, but felt they were wasting their time because they did not enjoy it. They preferred to be with women. The biggest obstacle in the lesbian's path to happiness is that black Africans do not easily adapt to anything new, and they think of lesbianism as an alien disease which can be got rid of only through brutality.

All lesbians have been through these problems in one way or another. Even gay men have an easier time than lesbians; they might be considered abnormal only because they are sometimes perceived to be born with both genders. The same thinking is not applied to lesbians. People think that women turn to lesbianism only when they are bored or when their relationships with men have gone sour. They do not want to accept that lesbianism exists; they ignore it, and their only thought is to punish it with brutality. To them, brutality is the only way of bringing lesbians back to 'normality' and of persuading them to get married.

The older generation is the least tolerant, and some think that they are being cheated by their daughters because if these daughters do not marry, the parents will not get rich with the bride price (*lobola*), which is paid to them by the groom.

Our generation cares less about what someone else is doing as long as it is her business. When people see something they do not like or that goes against the way they believe a person is supposed to act according to African culture, they pretend it is not happening and leave you alone. Some try and give you advice, but when they see it is useless they accept you as you are. In the workplace, where they know they cannot get rid of you, they just ignore you, and sometimes you feel that you do not exist as a person but as a robot, to be used or talked to only when it suits them. It makes us feel uncomfortable and threatens our confidence in ourselves. To make matters worse, to these male chauvinists, if you are black and a lesbian with no money they think your life is not worth two cents.

Life as a lesbian in Zimbabwe is difficult, and I do not know when people are going to wake up to the fact that we are as normal as the next person and that we require our rights. We cannot go into the streets' to demonstrate because that will mean being jailed. We only hope that one day in the near future we are going to be free and that people will accept and respect us as human beings. The truth is that people do not want to be realistic and accept us as members of the human race, but what can they do to change us? There is nothing that you can do or say to change a dove from cooing to barking, because it can never be a dog. The only way people can release their fury is by exterminating us or bringing us to the point of nervous collapse where some of us will end up committing suicide.

White lesbians in Zimbabwe are more fortunate, because some of their parents accept their sexuality, and 'he who has money is King'; so they are treated differently from the rest of us. All lesbians in Zimbabwe try and help each other, especially if they find out some of their friends are in trouble, but there will always remain those problems which are impossible for someone to solve. We wait patiently for the international (lesbian) community to assist us in gaining our rights. Even when we achieve them, the problem with black lesbians and their families will remain. We do not really know how to solve this, or how we can educate our families. Maybe, in the end, we will remain like this forever . . .

outraging public morality: the experience of a lesbian feminist group in costa rica[1]

rose mary madden arias

The background: how our group began

It was not until 1986–87 that the first efforts to form a lesbian feminist collective began in our country. The initiative was taken by a lesbian feminist, who, after participating in an international meeting of lesbians in Geneva, put the idea to us of forming a lesbian organization, so that we could get to know more about ourselves as lesbians, get rid of our feelings of guilt, and have our own space.

The fears and anxieties felt by lesbian feminists about making their sexuality known, even in private circles, made it very difficult to carry out this initiative. During the early meetings the majority of women felt that their sexuality was a private matter and there was no reason to become political publicly. Three women, however, took the decision to continue the process, and the lesbian feminist group Las Entendidas[2] was established in March 1987.

The dearth of information on lesbian feminism in the country, combined with the lack of feminist consciousness of the majority of lesbians and the latent fear of rejection by feminist groups, the women's movement and by society in general, created permanent obstacles to our project. Internalized anti-lesbianism, the inability to 'come out' and panic at the possibility of our sexuality being revealed, and the family and relationship consequences we supposed would result, led us to portray our organization as a 'support group'. We wanted to listen to each other and share our experiences of lesbian life. We did this with much pain because of the amount of imposed and self-repression.

Some of us had become involved in the activities of other feminist organizations. However, we could never totally identify with them because they never discussed the issues that weighed on us, such as the problems of lesbian mothers; the anti-lesbian attitudes of heterosexual feminists; discrimination at work; the image of lesbians projected by the patriarchy, etc. Even the support groups we participated in with heterosexual feminists always disregarded our sexuality and our daily lives with our partners.

Because of the danger we pose to the stability of the patriarchy, all its institutions ensure that we remain invisible, dispersed, guilty and homophobic. That is why, in order to be free and independent, we have to find our own identity as lesbians via the explanation of the patriarchal construction of society, which feminism has developed; we have to get to know ourselves in support groups, where our politico-erotic relationships with women can be openly shown and even encouraged. This need, expressed by a group of lesbian feminists, led us to search for a way of getting together. We looked for other lesbians who were not involved with feminist groups but had reached the conclusion that it was necessary to set up a group via other routes, and we began to meet. We did not really know which way to go, but the need to speak, to show each other affection and solidarity, meant we supported each other and this gave us the strength to act. We got together to read an article, to talk about intimate things, to express doubts and fears, and also to have a laugh.

We soon realized that our first struggle would be an internal one: to correct our poor sense of self-esteem, acquired in a society that rejected us; to resist those negative feelings we had towards ourselves, absorbed during a life of disrespect for our feelings; and to reject our passivity that made us tolerate the discrimination that we suffered in every area.

A very important action was our visible presence as a 'Lesbian Feminist Group' at the launch of Cladem-Costa Rica [Latin American women's rights network], the first time that a group had made a public appearance. It was significant, however, that in the list of participating organizations our name was changed and we appeared as a 'Group for Sexual Preferences'.

We proposed various stages in the life of our group. The first stage would be to emphasize the support nature of the group, in order to strengthen ourselves, to raise our self-esteem as lesbians and to rid ourselves of guilt. The next stage would involve making contact with other Costa Rican lesbians (feminist or not). The aim of the third stage would then be to relate to the Costa Rican feminist movement, after which we would move on to the fourth and final stage, namely coming out publicly to the rest of the women's movement and to society in general.

We made ourselves known to the lesbian community by various methods. We went to the bar 'La Avispa', almost the only public place at that time where lesbians could be themselves. We soon began to organize 'women only' nights, with activities aimed at raising our self-esteem. During those evenings, which took place on the last Wednesday of every month, we held talks on lesbian issues, organized poetry evenings, popular and classical music recitals, presentations of lesbian theatre and dance, painting and writing competitions. These nights showed us all that the more united we were, the better we could live and the better we could fight against the dominant heterosexism, a fundamental base of the patriarchy. We also began to publish a newsletter, giving information about relevant feminist activities both within the country and abroad, reproducing lesbian and feminist articles, and providing space in which lesbians could express themselves.

Remembering the Second Latin American and Caribbean Lesbian Feminist *Encuentro*[3]

Las Entendidas organized the Second Latin American and Caribbean Lesbian Feminist *Encuentro* in April 1990. We think it is important to report this event in detail, because its organization strengthened our group and provided very important theoretical feedback. The warmth of the event, the demonstrations of support and the response of many lesbians of diverse experiences, ages and situations, heartened the lesbian community. We shall also describe the manipulative action on the part of the press and some conservative sectors of our society opposed to the event, because it was precisely this campaign of rejection which had the positive result that lesbians were discussed at national level, and the public became aware that lesbian groups like Las Entendidas existed in the country.

After the first *Encuentro*, held in Mexico in 1987, Peru was chosen as the host country for the second conference. However, because of internal political problems in that country and given the repression let loose against homosexuals, it was considered too risky to use Peru as a location, so the organizers asked if it could be moved to Costa Rica. After contacts with GALF-Peru,[4] the idea of using Costa Rica as a host country took root more and more, and Las Entendidas was given the task of organizing the event.

The· aims of the *Encuentro* were: to develop the network; to exchange experiences; to consolidate a lesbian Latin American or Caribbean identity; to prepare a collective report for the Fifth Feminist *Encuentro* about to take place in Argentina; and to try and incorporate all women with Latin American roots.

Las Entendidas's first suggestion was that regional meetings be organized, grouping Central America, Mexico and the Caribbean in one block, and South America in the other. The appropriateness of this was debated, until it was finally decided to encompass the whole of Latin America and the Caribbean. By then, the group felt able to take on the responsibility for the *Encuentro*.

We decided to hold the event in April 1990 during Easter Week, because in most of our countries this would coincide with national holidays. We thought it would be easier for Latin American women to attend, as it was hardly likely that they would be given leave from work to attend a lesbian meeting. (The Mexican conference had been different in that immediately after the lesbian *Encuentro* the Fourth Latin American and Caribbean Feminist *Encuentro* was held.) We sent word to Peru that we had decided to take on the responsibility for organizing the *Encuentro*, and then contacted the organizers of the Mexican *Encuentro* to ask if they would send us information and money left from that first conference. At the same time, we asked them for help in publicizing the event among groups and individuals that might be interested in participating.

Taking advantage of the visit of one of the group to the USA, we contacted various lesbian organizations there. At that time, most of them had not heard of Las Entendidas, but we obtained a response and support from Las Buenas Amigas in New York, Mujerio (Women's Assembly) in San Francisco and from Conexus and GLU in Los Angeles. Thus, we ensured that information about the *Encuentro* would be circulated in lesbian and feminist circles.

With the almost immediate help of Las Buenas Amigas and the support of Las Entendidas, we had the financial means to continue organizing the conference. We also sought assistance from other groups, such as ILIS (International Lesbian Information Service) in Europe, and locally we approached several Costa Rican organizations in search of resources and support. The following stage involved distributing information about the *Encuentro* to addresses listed in the directory of the first conference. The magazine *Fempress*[5] also provided us with valuable advertising space.

Gaining moral ground?

The greatest difficulty that we came across was finding a venue. We needed somewhere that would provide privacy and at the same time be big enough to house 300 women and guarantee them a peaceful and friendly atmosphere, suitable for the intellectual, creative and leisure activities the *Encuentro* was offering. We changed the venue several times. On Thursday 22 March, the following article appeared in a national newspaper, *El Expreso*:

LESBIAN CONGRESS WILL BE HELD IN COSTA RICA

Groups are being organized to oppose on moral grounds the holding of a lesbian congress in Costa Rica in April. Further details of this strange event are not yet known, but it seems to be being organized from Chile, a country now seeing things that would never have been permitted before. It is only known that it will take place in the middle of next month in a still unidentified venue. Among opponents are law students at the University of Costa Rica, who have already contacted the Catholic Church as a first step.

Apart from the moral issues, as well as the damage to the country's image and to the upbringing of young people, the congress will begin on Good Friday, which shows disrespect for the religious customs of Costa Rica, according to its opponents. The fact that Costa Rica has been selected shows that we have women in this country who are totally defined in their aberration, to the extent that they are not afraid to display it, as happens in developed nations like the US, France, Spain or England.

If this congress is held, we are going to see how many ladies, including those who have held high positions, are encouraged to take part. A possible consequence from the congress being held is that soon the homosexuals who don't hide themselves like the *marimachas*[6] might come out like mad to hold their first congress as well.

IN OTHER COUNTRIES

In the US this kind of meeting is commonplace, to the extent that participants hold a march through the centre of the city where the event is being held. In these congresses they adopt resolutions demanding that lesbianism and homosexuality are seen as natural occurrences, therefore should be accepted as such and it is not fair to discriminate against them, even less to make fun of them. Among those that organize these events in other countries, and this should be made clear, are university teachers, many artists and intellectuals, and also a good number of civil servants.

In spite of our efforts to be careful and discreet about the date and location of the *Encuentro*, and to omit any compromising details, the newspaper *La Nacion* printed the following article:

LATIN AMERICAN ENCUENTRO: LESBIANS WILL MEET HERE

One hundred and fifty women from Latin America and the Caribbean will meet here between 23rd and 27th April for the 2nd Lesbian Feminist Convention. Members of a Costa Rican lesbian group called Las Entendidas, who asked for anonymity, stated that the idea of choosing our country was based on it being the country with the longest democratic tradition and with a tradition of respect for human rights and social liberty.

The participants, heterosexual and lesbian women together with AIDS specialists, social scientists and psychologists, will analyse a wide range of issues such as feminism and lesbianism, lesbian mothers, sexuality, leisure, addictions, and violence and repression, among others. While they did not reveal the venue, they said that it would be on a private country estate.

This lesbian reunion is not the first to be held in Latin America: another was organized in 1987 in Mexico. The idea for this kind of event came out of the Feminist *Encuentro* in 1985, given the need to study lesbianism more profoundly.

The Catholic Church and similar others, allied with the forces of repression and extreme right-wing groups, fought over the right to throw the first stone. The Catholic Archbishop launched the first attack, asking the authorities to ban the *Encuentro*:

The Archbishop of Costa Rica, Monseigneur Roman Arrieta Villalobos, denounced yesterday the holding of the II Lesbian Feminist *Encuentro* in Costa Rica. Through a press release to *La Nacion* the Prelate expressed the 'deep pain' he felt on finding out about the event. He lamented that at exactly the same time as the 'sublime mysteries of the Passion, Death and Resurrection of Our Lord Jesus Christ' the event would be taking place, 'revealing the institutionalization of a crisis of moral values'. At the same time he disapproved of any similar kind of get-together and requested that the relevant authorities use their powers to prevent it happening. 'Costa Rica has always been known for its human and spiritual values, and a meeting of this kind is a stain on the face of the country'.

So, controversy was let loose by the media, with tabloid treatment of the news ensuring that it made it to the front pages and caused a public scandal. The Minister of Administration ordered that while the conference was being held, 'women travelling alone [this meant unaccompanied by men] would not be allowed entry' to the country, as a preventative measure against the *Encuentro*.

It was then that we began to feel the full furious weight of sick patriarchal moralism. Our group became the scapegoat of Costa Rican Christianity. The war of nerves gained ground, tensions rising as the date of the *Encuentro* approached. Fears for our physical safety and that of the participants began to appear, with nothing but our intuition and good faith to deal with them. Although some argued for suspension of the event to prevent worse aggression, or suggested that it should be divided into small groups (i.e. to hold a reunion in disunion), the warmth and solidarity of women whose numbers increased daily, emerging ever stronger from the heated atmosphere in the country, resulted in the majority decision to go ahead with the event.

The *Encuentro* took place, albeit, in an atmosphere of great tension and aggression. But it was also an occasion of great solidarity from the participants. The pressure exerted on the group meant that some women dropped out, but for those of us who remained it only reinforced our conviction of the need to organize our strength as lesbians.

ACKNOWLEDGEMENT

Translated by Vivien Hughes.

EDITOR'S NOTES

1. This article is a shortened version of a paper presented at the Sixth Latin American and Caribbean Feminist *Encuentro* in El Salvador, in November 1993.
2. *Las entendidas*: those who know what one is about, who understand each other; used in Latin American countries as a synonym for lesbian.
3. *Encuentro*: conference, meeting, congress.

4. GALF: Grupo de Autoconsiencia Lesbianas Feministas; a lesbian feminist group which was based in Lima, but has since dissolved.
5. *Fempress*: Latin American journal distributed in many Latin American countries.
6. *Marimachas*: butch women, literally translated as 'masculine Marys'.

10 'todas locas, todas vivas, todas libres'[1]: chilean lesbians 1980–95

consuelo rivera fuentes

I dedicate this paper to all my anonymous lesbian sisters of LEA, whose names
I cannot mention for their own safety, particularly to the Jade Latina of my
lesbian wet dreams, to Leyla, Alejandra, Micky, Ivonne and Pecosa

When I was asked to write about the history of Chilean Lesbian organizations I accepted immediately, for two main reasons. First, because I do not
know of any written publication about this movement in English and
second, because as an out and proud Lesbian I want to contribute to the
growing visibility and subsequent acknowledgement of our human rights
as Lesbians in Chile. There is a long way to travel in this direction, and in
order to succeed we must be actively involved in making this hope a
reality; we need to become activists of our dreams and words, activists of
our lives and herstories.

People involved in the organization of activist groups which will be seen
as marginal and, more often than not, subversive, are usually more
concerned with how to solve the myriad of immediate problems that
setting up such a group brings, rather than considering the benefit of
writing a diary to record their group's history. When these marginal groups
(organized Lesbians in Chile may fall into this category) realize the
importance of speaking for themselves and do find the time to write about
their experiences, their accounts are completely denied, if not ridiculed,
by the media and official publications, which are the main and some
would say most effective instruments in the construction of sexist, heterosexual, militaristic and racist ideologies.

I have been away from Chile for three years at the moment of writing
this, so my knowledge of the Lesbian movement's present situation is
limited to what some friends can tell me on the phone or in letters. It is
difficult to start writing about the Lesbian herstory in Chile without

unintentionally omitting some events and names which have got to do with our birth, breathing, weaving and growing as a movement. So I shall begin this paper by narrating my own story of self-recognition, as a Lesbian growing up in a country with a long history of oppression and narrow social attitudes towards sex and sexuality. This process of self-recognition is not unique; on the contrary, it is very similar to that of other women growing up in the same country and times, so I hope that my account will give an overall idea of how we began to recognize and feel passion for ourselves and each other.

I then go on to describe the birth and growth of the first publicly known, but not acknowledged Lesbian organization – Ayuquelén. This is a brief description of the problems they had to face in coming out as organized Lesbians, but I do not feel qualified enough to go into details, because at the time of their birth I was involved in a different political arena. The more extensive coverage I give to the herstory of LEA from Concepción is due to the fact that I was a founder member, and therefore it is the organization I am most familiar with. Through the organization and development of this group, I happened to meet two of the founder members of Ayuquelén from Santiago. The aims of the two groups differ only on paper, and possibly the only differences between them were the initial reasons for their foundation.

In the section on LEA I narrate the origins of the group and how we came to redefine our Lesbian identities with a growing awareness of ourselves and each other as human beings who deserved nothing less than respect for our Lesbian right to be mad about each other, to be alive and to be free to determine the way we wanted to love and live. Finally, I give a limited overview of the situation of the group at the moment and conclude with a message to my Lesbian sisters of LEA, in which I ask them to Lesbianize their relationship with conventional political parties in order to continue being crazy, alive and free.

Wet dreams

I had my first conscious and distressing Lesbian fantasy when I was about twelve years old. The fantasy involved a very popular singer (Cecilia), whom I admired not only for her musical talents but because somewhere somebody had spread the rumour that this woman was a Lesbian. I did not have a clear idea of what the term meant or whether the rumours were true, but somehow I knew it was something I secretly liked and feared for the sexual desires that it aroused in me. I used to buy all her records, go to her recitals and then experience the most disturbing mental and often wet orgasms, which showed me that 'mental' was only a metaphor for real and fulfilling sexual desire. My room was full of her posters, and I would go through my adolescent life imitating her voice and style in my own singing, in local radio stations and at school. This was obviously more than admiration for a singer, and I now often wonder why my parents never seemed to notice. Was this because I had also started going out with boyfriends? Probably, but although I had several boyfriends and later married, these so-called 'deviant' feelings never left me. I used to fall desperately and secretly in love with some of my female friends and teachers, and later, when I began to have sex with men, I reached orgasm by imagining a woman's lips and body touching, licking and smelling my skin. My Roman Catholic upbringing[2] made me feel guilty, dirty and sinful as well as frightened all the time, and I tried to suppress the Lesbian inside, made myself believe that it was only a passing phase, when in fact I was a passing heterosexual.

I never accomplished the suppression of my sexual identity and, painfully, I used to look for signs from other women, to see if they had the same 'problem'. But I did not have the courage to actually ask them directly if they had so many disturbing doubts about their sexuality, and if they also shed lonely tears. Moreover, in the effort to hide my 'immoral' feelings I would laugh at stupid jokes about *maricónas* [queers] or *tortilleras* [pancakes], as Lesbians are derogatively called in Chile. Afterwards, in the almost safe space of my room, I would punish my cowardice by violently hitting my fists against the wall, punishing myself for failing to stand up to such homophobic remarks. Sometimes I would stay overnight with female friends, and lie awake without daring to move an inch in case they accused me of being a degenerate, dirty girl. My friends, most of them much younger than me, have told me that they went through a similar process, although their role models were the Argentinian singers Sandra Mihanovic and Celeste Carballo, who were out Lesbians in the mid-1980s.

In 1973 a military coup submerged Chile in a bloodbath and missing people for almost seventeen long oppressive years. Immediately after the initial shock, women began to organize themselves and to fight alongside men in an exhausting effort to overthrow the dictator.[3] I got involved in the struggle, and for some time I did not think of my sexuality; there were so many things to do, so many missing *compañeros* and *compañeras* to look for that there was no time to find myself, and I am certain that mine was not an isolated case. But from time to time, in the middle of a political meeting or demonstration, I would catch a look or feel another woman's hand stroking mine in a 'different' way. Somehow, somewhere deep inside myself, my instinct would tell me that this other woman was feeling more than comradeship, that her gentle touching was a passionate Lesbian one. Nevertheless, I always put those thoughts and feelings aside, either from sheer cowardice or a conviction that I was imagining things. What if I was getting the wrong message? So I always reacted by touching, hugging and kissing the other woman as I would do with any other *compañera* and continued passing as a heterosexual, 'happily' married woman while experiencing the most disturbing and delicious Lesbian wet dreams!

In 1983, I met the woman who was going to change my life. Because she was able to turn my silent dreams into concrete Lesbian love, I still call her 'the wonder woman'. For the first time, I was able to acknowledge that sexual desire and love for another woman were beautiful and had nothing to do with sin or guilt. However, letting go of my religious beliefs and attitudes took me some time, and it was not as sudden as this explosion of self-knowledge that came with my first real female-to-female orgasm. The reconstruction of my identity was not an easy task, as I had a son and centuries of patriarchal oppression behind me biting my heels. I knew now that I was a Lesbian and that I did not want to go back to having sexual love with men, but I still felt that I needed the illusory support that society could give me if I behaved like a 'proper' woman.

Almost a year passed before I came out to other people, mainly intimate friends. However, slowly but surely my recent acquired self-knowledge provided me with the courage and strength to assert my right to live and love as I wanted, with my Lesbianism always at the centre and giving me a different perspective and insight into the other parts of myself. My sexual identity had sex with all those different parts, licking, sucking, caressing and seeping through and inside them. My Lesbianism made love to my nationality and to my motherhood; it played tricks on my feminism and very often made me contradict myself, as it still does. My Lesbian inside became visible and tangible, and was – still is – always refusing to be made an invisible object again. That is why, for example, I call myself a feminist Lesbian and not a Lesbian feminist. I will, at this point, rebel against the 'stick-to-the argument' academic style of writing by digressing in order to explain my choice.

The word 'lesbian' can either be an adjective or a noun, depending on its position within a particular sentence or phrase. Take, for example, the phrase 'a lesbian feminist'. The core of the phrase is the noun 'feminist' and the word that defines this core (but which is not the centre) is the adjective 'lesbian'. In my view, women who identify themselves as lesbian feminists in this grammatical and linguistic context might be implying that the most important part of their self-definition is their feminism. An adjective, however determining, is always on the margin, almost invisible but not quite. I know that as a Latin American Lesbian in England I write from the margin, because society forces me into this marginalized position. However, I assert my right to be at the centre of my own self-definition. I want my identity to be more than just a peripheral adjective; I want it to be – and socio/linguistically I construct it as – a subject (myself), a verb (active/activating/activist) and a noun (in the centre of myself) as well as a defining/determining term. My choice, however linguistic, is a political subversion and that is why I write Lesbian with a capital L.[4]

After this necessary digression, and returning now to the issue of human rights violations during the dictatorship in Chile, the military rule also included Lesbians and gay men in their systematic killing and torturing of anybody who was thought to be subversive. We are subversive in that we refuse to accept that the conventional nuclear family is *the* only choice; moreover, we reject heterosexuality as *the norm*, although many of us, because of religion, family pressures, poverty and society in general, practise heterosexuality, or at some point in our lives have passed as heterosexual women, that is we have made people believe we are *normal*. Yet, sooner or later, our sexual orientation seeps through to the surface. When this surfacing takes place in the context of a dictatorship, many men and women who are sexual dissidents are killed or 'disappeared', tortured and/or raped, the former for not being *macho* men and the latter for being *amachadas*, that is, like *machos* in homophobic discourse – we cannot win, can we?[5] In Chile, when the so-called 'fathers of the nation' raped gay men, to cover up their own homosexual acts their solution was to kill, torture or make those gay men disappear. These 'brave soldiers and saviours of the nation' then accused us of being deviant when in fact it was *they* who were the degenerate ones. When they raped Lesbian women it was to punish us for having dared transgress the sexual boundaries set by fanatic heterosexual and militaristic ideologies. Some of us (both Lesbian and heterosexual women) who survived were left with 'children of the dictatorship', euphemistically speaking, and have had to bear the often innocent, but sometimes poisonous, question: how come you have this child when you claim to be a Lesbian?

While briefly a political prisoner in Concepción, I heard of another example of this cold and deliberate attempt to erase 'deviant' and 'subversive' women from our country. According to some of the people who came to visit us, when these 'honourable men' in Temuco (a city south of Concepción) wanted to unleash their evil sexual fantasies or simply have a laugh, they would force dogs to have sex with women, especially with those suspected of being Lesbians.

Despite these mass murders, tortures and discrimination, however, Lesbian women and gay men in Chile have managed to organize ourselves. That we sometimes have had problems between and within groups, mainly because of 'power trips', cannot be denied, but who does not have conflicts in their histories? The important thing is that we have made several attempts to organize ourselves, and back in Chile Lesbian and gay people are still facing discrimination bravely, becoming more and more sure of themselves and of their rights.

Ayuquelén

The Colectiva Lésbica-Feminista Ayuquelén started with a handful of women after a Lesbian woman was kicked to death in the early 1980s by a man who yelled *Lesbiana de mierda!* ['lesbian shit'] at her in the Plaza Italia, a well-known meeting place for marginal people, gay men and Lesbians, among others. The group began as an angry reaction to this murder, which was an obvious attempt to imitate and perpetuate the oppression we were experiencing at a more general level in the dictatorial society in which we lived. Political repression and sexual discrimination had resulted in an absence of women who could carry the Lesbian flag, so to speak, although I do not know of any Lesbian organization before that had done this, anyway. The women who began the group had originally belonged to various feminist groups, but they had grown tired of experiencing yet further discrimination: despite the common discourse between Lesbian and heterosexual feminists about gender oppression, the political urgency of the social mobilization to overthrow the dictatorship did not allow for a deeper analysis of different sexual options. The feminist movements of the time seemed to be very scared of having out Lesbians in their files. Being part of the women's movements with a feminist tint was bad enough (and punishable), and the media and other cultural and social organizations, official or not, thrived on the kind of stories which could distract the people from what was going on in the broader political arena. Imagine how subversive it was to have Lesbians in the movements! That, of course, could not be tolerated, as one of the counter-arguments used by patriarchy disguised in a military cloak was precisely that feminists were man-haters and Lesbians.

There came a moment when the Lesbian representation within the feminist movements in Santiago was strongly questioned, as Ayuquelén – which in the Mapuche voice means something like 'feeling or being happy'[6] – sought autonomy from the conventional political parties, which they felt were not giving enough space to reflect on women's issues, let alone Lesbian issues! After some disagreement precisely over this question of representation between Ayuquelén and the self-defined feminist organization La Morada, the group drifted apart for some time and was reduced to a mailbox number advertised in women's diaries. I do not have the exact details of what really happened between them, but I do know that after their separation from La Morada, and subsequent decrease in the number of members, only two brave women (Susana and Lili) kept the name and the mailbox in order to maintain contact with Lesbians who wrote to them from far away places in the long and narrow shape of our Chilean geography. I do not know what has happened to them since but they certainly set an example of Lesbian power and determination for many of us.[7]

Lesbianas En Acción

Some 500km south of where these events were taking place, and in the middle of a political turmoil after the first 'democratic' elections in about nineteen years, two women who worked at the University of Concepción launched a Women's Studies programme, which later, when recognized by the university authorities, turned into a Diploma in Women's Studies. As a student on this programme, the first module I studied was on domestic violence. At the end of the module everybody had to write a project on the topic, and I decided to investigate violence between Lesbians. Why did I choose to write about something that was in a way reinforcing the stereotypes about Lesbianism? Mainly for three reasons. Firstly, my partner at the time had told me about a previous lover who used to beat her, and I could not believe that this could happen between two women who had supposedly rejected patriarchal values, including violence. Secondly, the previous year I had met a young woman, Leyla,[8] and her woman lover, Alejandra, through the publication of my first book of poetry,[9] which had a Lesbian section (disguised, but not too much, for those other Lesbians wanting to come out). After a while I learned that they too were going through a violent phase. Thirdly, I wanted to challenge my own idealized notion of Lesbianism, in which everything was nice, 'rosy' and perfect because we were women who loved and made love to other women.

I want to narrate my first conversation and meeting with Leyla, because it illustrates how Lesbians learn to recognize each other in the most extraordinary ways, given certain circumstances. One day, after the publication and launch of my book of poetry, I received a phone call at the Institute where I used to work. The voice on the phone said nervously that she was an admirer of my poetry, that she had particularly enjoyed the last section of the book and could she have my autograph. Of course she did not really want my autograph; it was my first publication and the book was yet to be known by the so-called experts! I knew that she wanted to speak about the Lesbianism in my poetry but did not want to say it directly, just in case it was only in her imagination. I asked her why she liked that particular section, and she replied that it just described the way she felt, adding, 'I am one of the same'. I remained silent, because I did not want to put pressure on someone who was obviously very young and inexperienced. We arranged to meet in my office at work and I introduced her to my Lesbian lover. She was so delighted that the woman 'friend' who was with her was finally acknowledged as her partner. Although they had both noticed words and images of Lesbian love in my poetry, the poem that reassured them it was safe to come out to me was one in which I had 'hidden' the message A*mor Lesbiano, solitario femenino placer* (Lesbian love, solitary and feminine pleasure). Very few people, certainly not the 'experts', had noticed this game of mine. I had inserted this poem precisely with the intention that something like this would happen. The four of us have loved each other since then.

After writing my project, which was an academically weak but passionate analysis of the interviews and model of treatment I followed with Leyla and Alejandra, I asked if they would help me set up a group with the aim of offering a non-judgemental ear for other women who were experiencing similar difficulties. This was no easy task, because at the time both of my friends were trying to finish their degrees, and one of them in particular was quite apprehensive about meeting other women, and did not even feel comfortable with the word *Lesbiana* because of the negative connotations it has in our culture. I decided to go ahead on my own, and designed a very simple leaflet outlinging the aims of the 'group' and left them in public places. These aims included denouncing any form of discrimination and violence against women and acknowledging that violence can also exist between women; sharing our experiences as Lesbians and supporting each other in a sexist and heterosexist world. The leaflet concluded with a classic call to other Lesbians to break the silence (*rompe el silencio* was the slogan I used) by writing to a mailbox number that my best friend in the domestic violence module had kindly – and bravely – agreed to make public, so that we could arrange a safe meeting place. I must admit that I made it sound as if there were lots of women involved, and it worked! The first woman came to my house a few weeks later and after some minutes of conversation she showed me her right arm, which carried the scars of a knife injury inflicted by her married lover. I do not remember what we talked about, but I was so shocked by this experience that my initially weak attempt to create the group became a strong impulse.

In August 1991 (almost a year later) the group had acquired the name LEA, which stands for Lesbianas En Acción (Lesbians in Action). Alejandra designed a more artistic leaflet, which we handed out to women in the pedestrian precinct and at the entrance of the city's main post office. We received many dirty looks, but the result was that after about a month we held our first 'proper' meeting, attended by about six women. From then on the group grew steadily, attracting women from all sorts of class and educational backgrounds, ethnicities, beliefs and attitudes to Lesbianism, women's issues and feminism. Although there were obvious and sometimes gross class differences, what kept us together was our need to understand our sexual identities, to accept and love ourselves and each other and finally to break the isolation many of us had lived in for so long. Comments like 'we thought we were the only ones' or 'I know exactly what you have been through', were not uncommon.

At the beginning there was no set organization or agenda within the group, although almost everybody looked to me as the person responsible for the direction that we followed, possibly because the meetings were held in my house and because I was *la feminista* and the one who had started the group. Although this was not my idea of collectivity, I cannot deny that we needed somebody to deal with those issues that were considered difficult or boring, even funny, by others only because they had never thought seriously about them. Soon, however, others began to participate equally in the setting up of the group's agenda, suggesting and preparing topics for each of the sessions. That is how our initial aims started to change, and after a while we would talk not only about violence between Lesbian couples but also about Lesbianism and religion or Lesbianism in or out of the women's movements, about how some of them could not see themselves as feminists, and about funny experiences we had had in the course of coming out to ourselves and/or to others; we even did a workshop on self-defence, as one of the women had taken up karate at the time. Sometimes, when we could get hold of a Lesbian film (very difficult), and after a lot of sighs and laughter, we would attempt to discuss or analyse the film and our reaction to it. I particularly remember a session on Lesbians and their mothers and/or fathers, which reduced most of us to tears as we narrated our experiences. I have never felt such deep passionate love and understanding among Lesbians again: our tears were like silver cords which united us for ever – at least that is what I thought then.

This Lesbian love gave the group a sense of cohesion and solidarity which we could not have achieved if we had been involved in party politics, for example. We needed to grow *from and to* our inner selves before growing to the outside, which was the next step. I must say that not everything was as serious as it looks here. We had lots of parties, where we sang songs and danced with our lovers in a non-sordid, safe environment. Also, the size of the group within a big, but not that large city, would give rise to inevitable in-group relationships and arguments among the members of the group. Interestingly enough though, the internal cohesion was rarely affected by this.

LEA COMES OUT

The move outside the safe confines of our meetings came through an invitation made to the group from an organization called Cepss (Centro de Educación y Prevención de Salud Social y SIDA – Education and Prevention Centre for Public Health and AIDS), which wanted LEA to form a Lesbian section as, by then, only one woman (Micky) was attending meetings with young gay men in the organization, and she felt that most of the times the topics discussed in the meetings were not relevant to her own interests. Some of the women in the group were reluctant to attend the Cepss meetings, so we would still hold our weekly meetings at my home, but at the same time give some members of LEA the opportunity to expand their contacts. That is how Taller Ser (gay men in Cepss) and our group organized the First National *Encuentro* of Homosexual people in Coronel, a mining town near Concepción on the 1 and 2 of November 1991. Other groups that came from Santiago included Grupo Movilh and Las Yeguas del Apocalipsis, two creative radical gay artists. The latter, in an open, often acid and funny anti-discourse and in complicity with LEA and the *locas* (camp gay men), gave the grave homosexual men from Movilh, who were in a way repeating the old patriarchal formulas of party politics, more than a headache. LEA and Las Yeguas felt that the priority was 'to break the silence' about our right to Lesbianize or homosexualize our love for each other, but with total autonomy from political parties which had never acknowledged our sexuality.

After the *Encuentro*, LEA grew stronger and we held a series of programmes on a local radio station in which we read Lesbian poems, talked about our group and invited other Lesbian women to join us. Some members (only a couple of us were completely 'out') participated in open conferences and events organized mainly by Cepss to draw the attention of the general public to the problem of HIV/AIDS in Chilean society. And one woman who also belonged to the Partido Humanista de Chile [Humanist Party of Chile], attempted to raise awareness of Lesbian issues in her party, with the result that our group eventually agreed to vote in the local elections for those people from her party who promised to include Lesbian and gay issues in their political agenda. This was not a rejection of our belief in autonomy but rather a strategic and negotiated move.

In June 1992, posters announcing the First National *Encuentro* of Chilean Lesbians appeared on many walls of the capital, Santiago. The poster, designed by Alejandra from our group, depicted the profile of two naked women stroking each other, with the following verses adapted from one of my poems: 'Today I have danced with my sisters again/today I have had an orgasm without sperm/and my love has a woman's face' (translation from the Spanish). We decided, however, to put up the posters *after* the *Encuentro* for reasons of security. It would have been risky to put them up before, as we were unsure whether or not the now 'democratic' authorities would try to prevent the *Encuentro* from taking place. Although the congress was officially called by Ayuquelén, who by then had grown in numbers again and had acquired some foreign sponsorship to fund the event, the *Encuentro* was organized with the joint effort of Ayuquelén and LEA. The title of this paper has been borrowed from the invitation to the congress, which read: 'All of us crazy, alive, free: from our anonymous invisibility; with happiness, creativity and strength we invite you to participate in our First National *Encuentro* ... We will be waiting for you ... with affection and sorority ... Colectiva Ayuquelén, Santiago' (my translation).

The *Encuentro* meant solidarity, more coming out, organization and co-ordination between two groups which had been meeting for some time (LEA had invited Susana and Lili from Ayuquelén to do some workshops for us). The conference was attended by women from different regions of Chile, and we discussed those topics which we considered could determine our assertive insertion in an anti-Lesbian society: namely, self-esteem, Lesbian identity, feminism and its relation to Lesbianism. Some of the conclusions we drew from this congress were that we lived in a culture of prohibitions and that erotic Lesbian love did not only express itself in our sexual relationships but also in our work and everyday lives. We said that truth could not be legalized or our feelings 'normalized', and we concluded that since we were together in that *Encuentro* we were defining ourselves as organized and political Lesbians who wanted to get out of the ghetto and have our rights respected and acknowledged by the rest of Chilean society, especially by the women's movements. Five days later I flew to England.

LEA TODAY

A month before I left we had our first internal elections in LEA, as some feared that the group would disintegrate because one member was leaving. J., who belonged to the Humanist Party, was elected as the president and I believe that for a time everything ran smoothly. However, as one member comments, the group is beginning to change, as party politics undermine the collective and personal growth, as well as one of the original purposes, which was to break the silence as an organized Lesbian group and not as marginalized Lesbians within a political party, however inclusive this party claims to be. There have been 'power trip' problems, and suggestions that the name of the group be changed to Amazonas. This has resulted in internal divisions, in women leaving the group (there were around thirty-five when I left) and in an almost total cessation of work towards internal and personal growth. It seems that some members of the group are now covered with a 'humanist' flag instead of the Lesbian flag we wanted so much to carry collectively and freely.

A MESSAGE TO LEA

I ask LEA of today not to forget the lessons of the past, when women and men, inside and outside political parties, worked together to overthrow the dictatorship, but that once 'democracy' was reinstated, many women went back to the invisibility of their homes. As for those women who decided to stay in the public arena, you must know better than I do that they are finding it very hard, if not impossible, to put women's issues on the political agenda without being accused of putting *their* interests before *the people's*. I ask you: are women not people, are Lesbians not human beings? Remember the saying, 'Charity begins at home' and that only three years ago we attended our first national congress because we believed in *todas locas, todas vivas, todas* LIBRES.

We will never be free if we depend on the decisions of conventional political parties to give us some space. We will never be alive in a marginal dark room of their headquarters lent to us to keep us controlled, where they can use our energies, our creativity and our activism for their own interests. Their concerns might be as valid as ours, but they will never represent us in our Lesbian totality unless, as I said at the beginning of this paper, we continue to be the activists of our Lesbian dreams and aspirations. This does not mean that we cannot continue to negotiate with those political parties which are open to our Lesbian suggestions. They need us as we need them to improve the situation of Lesbians and gay men in Chile's legal and social systems, but we cannot give them power *over* us. Growth can take place inside and outside of us, but not *under* the cool shadow of structures which though, apparently open to change, nevertheless continually perpetuate sexist, racist and homophobic discourses in their search for power in public governmental hierarchies. Finally, remember what I once wrote on my bedroom door: *When Lesbians meet it is not only to 'sex' our passion for each other but most of all to Lesbianize our relationship with the world*. We broke the silence once, we can do it again.

NOTES

1. 'All of us mad, all alive, all free' could be the translation of this phrase. However, I must point out that *loca* in Spanish does not only mean mad in a negative sense – which could also be the case here, as anybody who trespasses the boundaries of rigid, set rules is considered crazy by society – but also indicates a positive, good attitude to life. It is also a term of love and affection.

2. At the age of seventeen I wanted to enter a convent and sometimes I wonder – and joke about it – whether unconsciously I just wanted to be in a female-only environment.

3. For a more detailed description of the Chilean women's movements during the dictatorship see: C. Boyle, 'Touching the air: the cultural force of women in Chile', in S. Radcliffe and S. Westwood (eds), 'Viva': Women and Popular Protest in Latin America (London: Routledge, 1993). J. Fisher, Out of the Shadows: Women, Resistance and Politics in South America (London: Latin American Bureau, 1993). E.Gaviola et al., Una Historia Necesaria: Mujeres en Chile: 1973–1990 (Santiago: Akí & Aora, 1994). C. Rivera, 'They do not dance alone: women's movements in Latin America's southern cone', in T. Cosslett et al., (eds), Women, Power and Resistance: An Introduction to Women's Studies (Oxford: Oxford University Press, 1995).

4. This does not mean that in other contexts I would not choose to use 'Lesbian' as an adjective, for example in the phrase 'Lesbian movements'. At the risk of repeating myself, I make use of this choice when it comes to my own self-definition.

5. The history of the mass murder of gay men under the Nazi dictatorship is an undeniable example of this type of human rights abuse. For more details and further reading, see: B. Adam, 'The Holocaust', in The Rise of a Gay and Lesbian Movement (New York: Twayne Publishers, 1995), pp. 49–59.

6. Gaviola et al., Una Historia Necesaria.

7. Ayuquelén has since revived and continues to be active on a national, Latin American and international level [editor].

8. Some names have been changed to respect the right of my friends to their anonymity.

9. C. Rivera, La Liberación de La Eva Desgarrada (Concepción: Editorial Aníbal Pinto, 1990).

11

las lunas y las otras

claudia csörnyei and silvia palumbo

The situation of lesbians in Argentina[1]

The position of lesbians in Argentina is not very different from any other country in Latin America. Ours is a system in which the neo-liberal model has succeeded with a high degree of political hegemony, in which recession condemns society, especially women, who are at the bottom of the productive system, to levels of mere survival. Ours is also a system in which the paralysis of justice allows corruption and fosters a feeling of impotence which translates itself into demobilization.

Ours is a society which has not lived under ten years of fierce dictatorship in vain. The fear of brutal repression, of a breakdown in the democratic system of government, of the suppression of constitutional guarantees, has been used by those in power to establish a perverse policy. It is perverse because attacks on, and blatant violations of, human rights remain unpunished. It is perverse because any challenge to the status quo is labelled as 'destabilizing', and the real victims of injustice find themselves accused of placing the system in danger. It is perverse because it declares itself open and pluralist, but, at the same time, establishes a scale of values in which minorities, discriminated against for class, gender, sexual orientation, ethnicity, religion, etc., are usually more violently oppressed as a result of the visibility we have won.

Our existence is not unaffected by the socio-economic and political framework we live in. Although in Argentina there is no legal body that explicitly punishes homosexuality and lesbianism, the police use a special mechanism called *edictos policiales*[2] to repress gay men and lesbians, taking them to police stations in order to check their criminal records. The major source of repression towards us, however, is the hypocritical attitude of the population: on the one hand, it shows itself tolerant and open; on the other, when a lesbian's appearance singles her out as 'different' from other women, hatred of us becomes a daily experience.

Although it is known that we lesbians exist (which is a cause for concern among the population), nobody sees us. However, this anonymity does not imply any protection, because by making our lesbianism invisible we show ourselves as we are not, creating a fiction in which we usually become trapped. Up to what point is the love of our families and friends for us or for the person they see? Up to what point does the fear of being sacked lead us to alienating acts? Up to what point can we stand the fear of being blackmailed by those who know and exercise power over us? Thus, the violence that covers our invisibility reveals itself through suicides, addictions and ill-treatment within our own love relationships.

DAILY LIVES

We women suffer from the imposition of a unique and 'normalized' model of sexual development. Any 'deviance from the norm' is automatically considered 'abnormal'. Therefore, we lesbians suffer every aspect of the oppression of women plus discrimination due to our sexual orientation. Such is the strength of this model that imposes heterosexuality on women as the only and almost obligatory option, that those who transgress this norm lose confidence in their own desires. Without anything to refer to, without spaces in which we can get together, without a culture that reveals our erotism, to be a lesbian means, for many of us, to be condemned to silence, self-marginalization and, solitude.

In relation to the family, the lesbians who are brave enough to show themselves as such to their parents, sisters, brothers and friends, are few. The fear of not being loved, of causing pain or disillusion, of not being able to fulfil what is expected of them, is sometimes so powerful that they prefer to hide their lesbianism. There are few emotional attachments which truly accept and support a woman who reveals her lesbianism.

Discrimination at works exists as well. Although there is an anti-discrimination law in Argentina, it is hardly ever enforced. Cases where lesbians have been sacked because of their sexuality have been explained away by other reasons. And when lesbianism is the indisputable motive, the lesbian herself prefers to forget the matter in order to avoid her lesbianism being publicly exposed. In the legal field, the lack of protection is total, and the situation of lesbian mothers regarding the custody of their children is particularly critical.

In relation to health, we lesbians are completely helpless: firstly, because of a lack of information concerning the risk factors for lesbians in regard to HIV/AIDS, secondly, due to fear of prejudice and in the face of ignorance from health staff regarding lesbianism (gynaecological consultations are inaccurate both in their diagnosis and treatment), and thirdly, because of cruel or erroneous psychological treatment, again due to lack of support or knowledge of lesbianism.

On the social level, despite the supposed openness towards us, personal emotional problems, such as the lack or loss of a partner, family pressures, work and financial situations, are experienced with a great amount of pain and loneliness. Pubs and discos remain the only meeting places for lesbians. For many these are the only public spaces in which their lesbianism has been accepted. However, a high consumption of alcohol is promoted, access to drugs is facilitated, and so many of the problems of the lesbian community are exacerbated (internalized anti-lesbianism, ill-treatment between lesbians, self-destructive behaviour, stigmatization, and ridiculing those who do not subscribe to certain codes of behaviour, etc.). Although they allow many lesbians to meet each other, and to discover that they are not the only ones loving other women, it is true that in such places the possibility of self-development, self-affirmation, reflection, creativity and self-esteem are scarce. This situation created the need for new and different spaces in which we could get together, exchange experiences, seek information, promote our creativity and find support for our problems and anxieties.

POLITICAL ORGANIZATION

The only organized group in Argentina are to be found in Buenos Aires. There is a high turnover of participants and the majority join seeking support rather than because they want to get involved in political work.

Gay men are deeply misogynous, and this makes it difficult for lesbians to participate in so-called mixed groups. Many of these groups are run by men, and their agendas, anxieties, contents and procedures are mainly masculine, making the specific characteristics of lesbianism invisible even for those women taking part in such groups.

There are lesbian activists in feminist groups, together with heterosexual women. Many of them accept their own lesbianism and include lesbian issues in their groups' agendas, while others hide their lesbianism, not only from heterosexual feminists (the presence of lesbians is still badly regarded within the feminist movement) but also from out lesbians, although sometimes they are supportive out of 'solidarity'.

Job insecurity and long working hours, crucial for economic survival, undermine political activism among lesbians. All political work is voluntary and carried out during spare time. None of the lesbian groups has its own venue. This wastes a lot of time, as they constantly have to look for new places in which to work. It also makes it difficult to attract new lesbians, who now have to depend on mailings or just chance to find existing groups.

We lesbian activists are at the stage of getting together, getting to know each other, and forming a community. Because of this, our main tasks at the moment are the reflection and exploration of our own diversity, to study and to communicate. The spaces we are occupying within the women's and feminist movements are, for now, the places where we can develop ourselves.

Lesbian feminism in Argentina

Lesbian feminism has existed in this country since feminism was first considered and debated. However, feminist activism developed within groups formed by both heterosexual women and lesbians, and, almost as a tradition, its specific demands have been achieved without reference to lesbian issues. Many lesbians did not come out, and those who did have to struggle against the anti-lesbianism of co-activists. Whether due to fear of being 'mistaken for lesbians', or because the priorities under consideration were other than lesbian, heterosexual Argentinian feminists did not usually see the presence of lesbians within the feminist movement as positive. However, and despite the fact that they were deliberately excluded, many lesbian activists feel ourselves to be feminists, though not all declare it explicitly.

Although we can speak about an incipient lesbian movement, it is clear that we cannot label it as feminist. This is not because we are not feminist, but because the few channels of participation provided by heterosexual feminists have thrown up so many obstacles for lesbians that many prefer alternatives. They agree with the general ideology but question the practice by Argentinian feminists (notwithstanding honourable exceptions that prove the rule).

Finally, there has not been a profound debate about the relationship between feminism and lesbianism. We can assert that, despite the fact that there have been and still are lesbian feminists, a lesbian feminist movement has not been built. To try to find an explanation for this could get us tangled up in very recent and almost contemporary history. What it is true, though, is the fact that lesbians have worked both in lesbian (recently) and feminist fields, despite the fact that within the latter their participation has not been sufficiently committed to their lesbian activism.

The publication in 1987 of the journal *Cuadernos de Existencia Lesbiana* (*Notes on Lesbian Existence*), edited by a small group of lesbian feminists, together with the Fifth Latin American and Caribbean Feminist *Encuentro*, held in November 1990 in San Bernardo, Argentina, offered us the opportunity of meeting other lesbian feminists, and opened the door to the creation of new groups. For several reasons few of these groups remain. The lesbian groups currently working are: Convocatoria Lesbiana (Lesbian Call); Las Lunas y Las Otras; Madres Lesbianas; Sentimiento; the women in CHA (Homosexual Community of Argentina) and in SIGLA (Argentinian Society for Gay and Lesbian Integration). Another very important organization is the Frente de Lesbianas de Buenos Aires (Buenos Aires Lesbian Front), which is a coalition of groups and individual lesbians who, having certain basic agreements, work together on specific activities.

Las Lunas y Las Otras

ORIGINS OF THE GROUP

The group was formed on 13 July 1990, growing out of a women's writing workshop which many of us were attending. We got together spontaneously because of the need to create a space in which we could tell our own stories, where we could strengthen ourselves against daily discrimination, and where getting to know the others could enlighten our own self-knowledge.

After many years and few precedents, a group of lesbian feminists had finally been created in Argentina. And the Fifth Latin American and Caribbean Feminist *Encuentro* received us as such, with the anticipated commotion that was provoked by declaring ourselves lesbians and feminists in a country which had suffered so many years of repression and censure.

During the first two years we studied and discussed articles, films, books of fiction and essays about feminism and lesbianism. The group was composed of a stable number of members, and we did not carry out activities in the community except to participate in events and meetings organized by the feminist and women's movements. We frequently organized open meetings in order to debate specific issues, which lesbians from other groups or individual lesbians used to attend.

Gradually, Las Lunas y Las Otras started to acquire a certain identity, a particular view of the world, of the situation of women and, especially, of lesbians. Each of us integrated her lesbianism into her daily life, and, at the same time, felt the need to change her life in order to make her lesbianism and that of others more visible.

By 1992, Las Lunas y Las Otras had already achieved the characteristics of a group. Within it co-existed (sometimes pacifically, sometimes passionately) diverse points of view on the issues we were involved in. The possibility of dissenting, and at the same time maintaining a certain group cohesion, often caused difficulties which were, in turn, a source of development. It was at this time that the name of our group (chosen almost by chance) made real sense. Our 'moon' [*la luna* – female in Spanish] unequivocally alludes to women, but is trying to break the hierarchical assumptions of gender present in our culture in relation to the 'feminine'. We wanted to re-signify the moon, allowing her command of all her phases (a moon can be new and full, waning and crescent). And, additionally, we wanted to have the opportunity to choose not to be 'moons', but to be the 'others' [*otras*]. Our name was successful in describing the group: it had created an image of ourselves which was becoming clearer and more certain, and at the same time, this image was flexible enough to assimilate the diversity, the turnover of participants, the horizontality, the taking of decisions by consensus and the absence of fixed roles.

We were no longer just a group of friends united by a common cause, we had forged our own collective discourse, using our own experiences as a starting point, and this gave us back our confidence, lost in the web woven by the heteropatriarchy. We did not have the answers to all the questions, but we stopped looking outside for an explanation that could justify ourselves, because we understood that there was nothing to justify. Only we could speak about ourselves. And when we could name ourselves, when we could acknowledge ourselves, the next step was the need to know the name of other lesbians.

ACTIVITIES AND POLITICAL PARTICIPATION

After attending meetings, assemblies and conferences organized by the feminist and women's movements, and having passed through the experience of becoming visible, we considered ways of communicating with other lesbians, hidden in their homes, disconnected from each other, without spaces for themselves. So, the Jornada de las Lunas: 1er Encuentro de Lesbianas (Day of the Moons: First Lesbian *Encuentro*) was held in Buenos Aires, in August 1992. We went through our address books, and those of our friends, to organize a nationwide network of communication in order to publicize an event which, until that moment, was unheard of in the country. In spite of the insecurity, the doubts and the uncertainty, seventy lesbians got together that Sunday. We discussed, meditated, cried, and agreed that to be a lesbian involves much more than just sexual orientation. We lived that day within an atmosphere of profound solidarity, working in different workshops, and expressing ourselves artistically within the framework of an open radio station.

Thus another phase had began for the group. Now we were known by the lesbian community, and we became the reference point for many, given the vacuum caused by the anti-lesbianism of the feminist movement and the mainly patriarchal and misogynous attitude of the mixed lesbian and gay groups.

The communication by mail between lesbians in Buenos Aires and those in the interior of the country intensified. We were often invited to participate in the mass media, but we appeared only in situations where we could control the message and in spaces run by women (radio, newspapers, alternative magazines, cable TV, etc.).

In November 1992, one of us participated in the First South American Lesbian and Gay *Encuentro*), held in Chile by the Comité de Servicio Chileno Cuáquero (Chilean Quakers Service Committee), a branch of the American Friends Service Committee. Since then, the communication with lesbian groups in Latin America and the Caribbean has become more fluid, and the exchange of information, news and materials means we can keep in touch, widen our horizons and learn about other realities.

1993 was a very productive year for Las Lunas y Las Otras because we organized the Second Lesbian *Encuentro*, and we were able to carry out a long-desired project: the publishing of our journal, which is meant to be semestral but, due to the scarcity of our resources, we publish it when we can. We created and presented workshops on lesbophobia within the

Eighth National Women's *Encuentro*, and within the First National Women's Health Network *Encuentro*. We also co-ordinated several study seminars for lesbians from a lesbian feminist perspective, either in hired venues or in our own homes. We became aware that as well as our aim of bringing lesbians together, we should recover their words, artistic productions and their stories. So we decided to record everything that was said within the groups in order to keep such rich material as a real support for our lives. We also categorized all the material accumulated during these years, creating a Lesbian Feminist Library, which is open to all the lesbian community, and contains both literary and theoretical texts.

In May 1994, we called the Third Lesbian *Encuentro*. Some of the women who had been present at previous conferences organized and chaired their own workshops, thus achieving women's self-management. In the same year we were invited to Lima, together with nine other lesbian groups from different Latin American and Caribbean countries, to draft a joint report about lesbianism for presentation at the Regional Preparatory Forum of Non-Governmental Organizations (September 1994 in Mar del Plata, Argentina), that led up to the United Nations World Conference on Women, held in Beijing in 1995. Although Las Lunas y Las Otras is not a member of ILGA (International Lesbian and Gay Association), we were also invited to their Annual Conference in New York, and to the Stonewall 25 celebrations.[3]

We continue to participate in the Frente de Lesbianas de Buenos Aires, and we organize a number of activities under that umbrella. Among these was the organisation of the Fourth Latin American and Caribbean Lesbian Feminist *Encuentro*, held in Argentina in April 1995.

Apart from being part of the Latin American and Caribbean lesbian feminist network, we have contacts with lesbians in the USA, Canada, Germany and the UK. We have started a lesbian publishing house, which will publish fiction and theory produced mainly by lesbians from our country, the rest of Latin America and the Caribbean. Recently, Las Lunas y Las Otras has received approval for two projects. The first is a year's funding to pay the annual rent of a house, which will allow us to have our own space to carry out our own and other groups' activities. The funds were granted by the Comité Mundial del Día de la Oración de las Mujeres (World Committee of Women's Prayer Day). The second involved funds thankfully received from the Frauen-Anstiftung, Germany, for a Documentation Centre, equipped with a computer and a printer.

We would like to conclude by stating that the opinions expressed in this article do not, of course, represent those of all Argentinian lesbians. The preparations for Beijing (from which the majority of Argentinian lesbians withdrew) and the Fourth Latin American and Caribbean Lesbian Feminist *Encuentro* caused big discussions around representation on the part of certain activists, and around the possible institutionalization of the Latin American lesbian movement and the resulting danger of losing autonomy. It is for these reasons that we would like to make clear that what is presented here is exclusively our point of view. Many other voices could tell our story, ours is just one of them.

ACKNOWLEDGEMENT

Translated by Vivien Hughes.

NOTES

1. For the first part of this article, we have used the *Informe de Situación de las Lesbianas en la Argentina* (*Report on the Situation of Lesbians in Argentina*), written by the Frente de Lesbianas de Buenos Aires, 1993.
2. *Edictos policiales*: 'Edicto Escándalo: Art. 2 Inc. F: 'Those who exhibit themselves in public dressed or disguised as members of the other sex'. Art. 2 Inc. H: 'Persons from one or the other sex, who publicly incite or offer themselves for sex acts'. Art. 2 Inc. I: 'Those subjects publicly known as perverts who are found with people under eighteen years old'.
3. Anniversary of the Stonewall riots in 1969 that took place after the police raided lesbian and gay bars, notably the Stonewall Bar, in Greenwich Village, New York City. This date is said to mark the birth of the lesbian and gay movement in the USA [editor].

*r*esources

The groups listed are autonomous lesbian feminist groups unless indicated otherwise.

Asia and Pacific Islands

ALN Nippon
c/o Regumi Studio Tokyo
JOKI. Nakazawa Building 3F
23 Arakicho
Shinjukurku
Tokyo 160
JAPAN

Sakhi
B-44 Defence Colony
New Delhi
110 024
INDIA
Tel/Fax: +91 11 4628970

CLIC
PO Box 2356
CPO, Quezon City 1163
PHILIPPINES
Fax: +632 911 6239
E-mail: clic@phil.gn.apc.org

Anjaree
PO Box 322
Rajdamnoen
Bangkok 10200
THAILAND

ALN Taiwan
PO Box 7–70
Taipei 106
TAIWAN

Chandra Kirana
PO Box 6525 JKSDW
Jakarta 12065
INDONESIA

Africa

FLOW
PO Box 23297
Joubert Park 2044
Johannesburg
SOUTH AFRICA
Tel: +27 11 982 1016
Fax: +27 11 339 7762

SISTER Namibia
PO Box 40092
Windhoek
NAMIBIA
Tel: +264 61 230618/230757
Fax: +264 61 236371
(heterosexual/lesbian)

Latin America

El Closet de Sor Juana
Apartado Postal 25–392
Mexico D.F. 03421
MEXICO
Tel/Fax: +55 5 519 7063

Las Entendidas
Apartado 1057
San Pedro Montes de Oca
San Jose
COSTA RICA

Colectiva Ayuquelén
Casilla 70131
Correo 7
Santiago
CHILE

Colectiva LEA
Casilla 681
Correo Concepción
CHILE

Las Lunas y Las Otras
Casilla de Correo 21
Sucursal 53(B)
1453 Buenos Aires
ARGENTINA

La Media Luna
Apartado Postal 3361
Centro de Gobierno
San Salvador
EL SALVADOR

Um Otro Olhar
Caixa Postal 51540
01495-970 San Paulo
BRAZIL

International

International Lesbian Information
Service
c/o COC
Nieuwezijds Voorburgwal 68–70
1012 SE Amsterdam
THE NETHERLANDS
Tel: +310 20 623 1192
Fax: +310 20 626 7795

International Gay and Lesbian Human
Rights Commission
1360 Mission Street
Suite 200
San Francisco
CA 94103
USA
Tel: +1 415 255 8680
Fax: +1 415 255 8662
E-mail: iglhr@igc.apc.org
(gay/lesbian)

*i*ndex

Pan Africanist Congress (PAC) (South Africa) 103
parody 73
'pars' 36, 37, 47, 48, 49
Partido Humanista de Chile 148, 149
Parvati 62–3
'peng-kids' 73
Peru 132, 159
Philippines, the 4, 31–53, 76
    lesbian groups 2, 4, 40, 46–7, 52–4
    sackings of lesbians in 2, 52–3
pink triangle 15
Pink Triangle (Malaysia) 82, 83
'PK' 73
poetry 30, 109–10, 144–5, 148
policing 34, 36, 79–80, 120, 152–4
    by lesbians 48, 74, 154
    see also legislation
political parties 51–2, 53, 104, 144, 148, 149
Population and Development, International Conference on *see* United Nations
possession 58
postmodernism/post-structuralism 73, 83
Prayer Day, World Committee of Women's 159
pregnancy and choice of lesbianism 74
priorities 11, 60, 64, 75, 98–100, 101, 113–14, 116
prisoners of conscience 15
prisons 16, 19, 107, 142–3
privacy 25, 63, 68, 118
    see also space
'promiscuity' 79–80
psychiatry/psychiatric treatment 16–17, 18, 24, 90, 118, 154
psychoanalytic theory 90
public space *see* space
publishing 93, 159
punishments 11–18, 57–9, 63, 77, 78, 80, 129

Quakers 158

'race' and racism 1, 6, 7, 16, 72, 99
    and anti-lesbianism 6–7

immigration legislation and 18
    lesbian groups and 99, 100, 101
rape 19, 59, 80, 88–9, 123, 125, 142, 143
refugees 17–18, 115
representativeness, issues of 7–8, 70, 159–60
reproductive health issues 89
reproductive rights 50
residence rights *see* immigration
resistance 4, 121–2
    see also feminism
resources 8, 110, 158–9, 161–2
Rich, Adrienne 28
Rig-Veda 68
Rivera Fuentes, Consuela 7, 138–43, 144–6, 149
role-playing *see* butch/femme
Roman Catholicism *see* Catholicism
Romania 15, 17, 18
Roth, Claudia 20
rural contexts *see* urban/rural differences
Russia 17, 18

sackings 2, 52–3, 153
safe sex 50, 78, 80, 111
'sakhi' 64, 69
Sakhi (New Delhi) 12, 64–9
Samson, Laura 54
Sappho 10
Sarabia, A. L. 30
Save the Children Fund 2
Scandinavia 17
    see also individual states
Scholinski, Daphne 24
security 74
self-criticism, Maoist 51–2
Sentimiento (Argentina) 156
separatism, lesbian 45
Sevilla, Rebacca 28
sex (gender) *see* gender
sex/sexual behaviour 47, 60, 68, 91
    and definitions of lesbians/lesbianism 71–2
    definitions of 3
    safe 50, 78, 80, 111
sex change 58–9, 73
    see also transsexuals
sex education 111

see also safe sex
sexuality, construction/formation of 48,
        67, 74–5, 92
    see also choice
Sharia see Syariah law
Shiv 62–3
SIGLA (Argentinian Society for Gay and
        Lesbian Integration) 156
Sin, Jaime 39–40
single mothers 111
SISTER Collective (Namibia) 110, 116
SISTER Namibia 2, 110, 116
sisterhood 46
Sisters of Mercy 119–20, 121
Sobritchea, Carol 54
social pressures 67–8, 111–12
    see also policing
South Africa 1, 3, 5–6, 8, 18, 98–105, 112,
        116
    apartheid system 99–100, 105–6 108
        struggle against 98–100, 101
        terminology of 105–6
    Constitution 5–6, 23, 24, 103, 104–5
    lesbian groups 99, 100–1
    and Namibia 114–15, 117
    and UN Beijing Conference 23
South African Communist Party 103
space
    public 60, 64–5
    victim 60
    women-only 61, 62–3
    see also privacy
Spain 18
spirits 3, 118–19, 121–2
state, oppression of lesbians by 88, 91,
        92–3, 94
    see also legislation
Stonewall 159
Sughandi, Mien 86
suicide and suicide attempts 11, 65, 119,
        120, 129, 153
SWAPO (South West Africa People's
        Organization) 112–14, 116
    Women's Council 113
Sweden 18, 20
Syariah law 12–13, 14, 78

't–bird' 36, 37

Taller Ser 147
Tarulata 58–9
terminology 2–4, 60, 87, 89, 92, 106, 140,
        141–2
    see also lesbianism/lesbians, self-
        definitions and words used
Thadani, Giti 26
Thailand 12, 45, 76
therapy/therapists see counselling;
        psychiatry
'third sex' 36, 37, 90
Tity Koesomodardo, R. A. 86
Toksvig, Sandi 2
tolerance and myths of tolerance 61, 62,
        63
'tomboys' 36, 37, 73, 76
torture 16, 19, 142, 143
    see also violence
transsexuals 77, 86, 90
    see also sex change
Trinidad and Tobago 15
Tswete, Steve 104
Tunisia 15

UDF (United Democratic Front) (South
        Africa) 101, 102
UK see United Kingdom
unemployment 111–12
United Democratic Front (South Africa)
        101, 102
United Kingdom 2, 17, 28, 73
    immigration to 17, 18
    legal situation 11–12, 15, 19
    studies of lesbians in 11, 16, 27
United Nations
    First World Conference on Women
        (Mexico, 1975) 23
    Third World Conference on Women
        (Nairobi, 1985) 23
    Fourth World Conference on Women
        (Beijing, 1995) 7, 20–6, 44–5
    preparatory meetings and
        documents 10, 90, 91–2, 159–60
    Human Rights Committee 25
    International Conference on
        Population and Development
        (Cairo, 1994) 14, 39–40, 50, 94
    and SWAPO 112